PATRIK IAN MEYER

THE 4 PILLARS OF CRITICAL THINKING

103 TECHNIQUES & HACKS
TO IMPROVE YOUR WORK AND PERSONAL LIFE
BY MASTERING MENTAL SKILLS

© Copyright 2023 - All rights reserved.

The content contained within this book may not be reproduced, duplicated, or transmitted without direct written permission from the author or the publisher.

Under no circumstances will any blame or legal responsibility be held against the publisher, or author, for any damages, reparation, or monetary loss due to the information contained within this book, either directly or indirectly.

Legal Notice:

This book is copyright protected. It is only for personal use. You cannot amend, distribute, sell, use, quote, or paraphrase any part of this book's content without the author's or publisher's consent.

Disclaimer Notice:

Please note that the information contained within this document is for educational and entertainment purposes only. All effort has been executed to present accurate, up-to-date, reliable, and complete information. No warranties of any kind are declared or implied. Readers acknowledge that the author does not render legal, financial, medical, or professional advice. The content within this book has been derived from various sources. Please consult a licensed professional before attempting any techniques outlined in this book.

By reading this document, the reader agrees that under no circumstances is the author responsible for any direct or indirect losses incurred as a result of the use of the information contained within this document, including, but not limited to, errors, omissions, or inaccuracies.

Table of Contents

Introduction 7

Pillar 1: Foundation 11

Chapter 1: Definition 15
    What Is Critical Thinking? 15
    Why Is Critical Thinking Important? 16
    Critical Thinking vs. Other Types of Thinking 18
    Benefits of Critical Thinking in the Real World 19

Chapter 2: Models 23
    Proximate vs. Root Cause 24
    Cognitive Bias 29
    Hanlon's Razor 36
    A Brief Historical Perspective 37
    How Hanlon's Razor Is Applied 37
    Common Criticisms of the Razor 38

Chapter 3: Skills Needed 41
    Observation 42
    Analysis 43
    Interpretation 44

Inference 45

Evaluation 46

Communication 47

Problem-Solving 49

Pillar 2: Process 51

Chapter 4: Identify the Problem or Issue 55

Chapter 5: Research, Opinions, and Arguments 59

The Kinds of Sources 60

Evaluating the Quality of Sources 62

Chapter 6: Analyze the Arguments 65

The Structure of Arguments 66

Arguments vs. Non-Arguments 67

Chapter 7: Identify Assumptions and Biases 69

Defining Assumptions and Biases 70

Common Areas of Bias 71

How to Avoid Making Assumptions and Biases 77

Chapter 8: Evaluating Data 83

Reliability of the Data 84

Significance and Relevance of Information 85

Relationship Between Evidence and Claim 86

Weighing Competing Evidence and Information 88

Chapter 9: Draw Conclusions or Solutions 95

The Purpose of Drawing Conclusions 96

Factors that Influence Solution Generation 97

The Stages of Drawing Solutions 98

Pillar 3: Improvement 105

Chapter 10: Self-Reflection in Critical Thinking 109
Why Self-Reflection Is Important 110
Areas of Focus in Self-Reflection 112
Tools for Self-Reflection 115

Chapter 11: Role of Diverse Perspectives 119
Barriers to Diverse Perspectives in Critical Thinking 120
Incorporating Diverse Perspectives into Critical Thinking 122

Chapter 12: Critical Thinking Exercises 125
Working on Puzzles 125
Reading Critically 127
Participating in Discussions or Debates 129
Solving Practical Problems 131

Pillar 4: Application 133

Chapter 13: Applying Critical Thinking in Daily Life 137
In Health and Wellness 137
In the Workplace 138
In Education 139
In Personal Finance 140
In Personal Relationships 141

Conclusion 143
Glossary 145
References 149

Introduction

In today's world, it is easier than ever to access information and make decisions with the assistance of technology. Almost everyone relies on the latest gadgets, which provide valuable information and knowledge at the touch of a button. While this is good, reliance can also decrease our ability to think critically. With so much information accessible and presented in such a straightforward format, it can be tempting to take whatever is given without assessing its validity and relevancy.

This reliance on technology and ready-made solutions can leave us less incentive to consider problems and develop their original solutions. Subsequently, we accept answers without critically examining them first. For example, when presented with multiple possible solutions to a problem, we may choose the most popular or most convenient option without analyzing the pros and cons of each choice. This culture of convenience is dangerous as it can potentially be disempowering. Additionally, the sheer amount of information accessible through technology can lead to information overload. As such, evaluating data, searching for new sources, or engaging in further research can leave us overwhelmed, confused, and unenthused. This "laziness" or disregard for critical thinking has displaced serious consideration and replaced it with a reliance on technology to make decisions on our behalf.

In the long run, this lack of critical thinking skills can have serious consequences as our ability to analyze and make thoughtful decisions decreases. Without thinking outside the box, we may be unable to make wise decisions in more complex matters. Likewise, this lack of insight can leave us vulnerable to misinformed opinions and dangerous actions.

Meanwhile, critical thinking allows us to evaluate information, analyze facts, and interpret data. This skill helps us develop insights and draw conclusions rather than relying on the opinions and beliefs of others. Likewise, critical thinking allows us to assess different perspectives, weigh evidence, and investigate various arguments. From that, we could come up with informed and well-reasoned decisions. Critical thinking also encourages us to be mindful and reflective of our biases and preconceptions. This way, we can challenge our beliefs and create an open-minded environment for learning. Through this process, we can better understand complex subjects and gain deeper insight into our opinions.

Thereupon, this book contributes to promoting critical thinking in the modern era. Consider this book your new best friend in improving your critical thinking skills. Through easy-to-understand facts and proven techniques, this book will teach you the foundational tools you need to face everyday problems with confidence and honesty.

As you read it, you will understand the steps necessary to understanding life in ways you may have never done before. Aside from that, it will let you see the world more clearly and vividly. This book will also guide you through becoming an active observer of all the information life throws your way. You will find 103 techniques, tips, and strategies on how to analyze complex ideas as you view the world critically. It's peppered throughout the book, and it's intentionally designed this way to serve as your guide along each step of the process. Soon, you can analyze complex topics, weigh ethical questions, and make sound decisions.

In the pages ahead, you will find a wealth of knowledge to gain more insight into how the world works. Plus, you will discover how to build your foundation of analytical thinking, as well as strengthen your problem-solving abilities and hone your logical reasoning skills. With this book, you will develop the necessary tools to take full control of your life and begin achieving the results you desire.

Neglecting to think critically can derail your progress and set you behind in life. But, with the help of this book, you can understand the concepts related to critical thinking. As such, it will break down the largest issues into smaller components, making it easier to comprehend them. This practical guide will also introduce four pillars that make up the structure for improving your critical thinking skills. With each pillar's contents, you will unlock the power of reasoning and logical thought.

The four pillars of critical thinking provide tools for individuals to think with greater clarity, accuracy, and logic. Pillar one, foundational skills, focuses on fostering the abilities required for critical thinking. For instance, it will discuss analytical reasoning, problem-solving, and creative expression. Meanwhile, the second pillar looks at processes that help discern and evaluate a situation to reach informed conclusions. Then the third pillar is devoted to improving our thought process to make more reliable decisions and better assessments. Finally, the fourth pillar calls for applying these learned techniques in real-world scenarios. As such, it includes making sound choices and resolving issues effectively.

There are many ways through which critical thinking can create an impact on a person's life. As you get deeper into the book, you will learn more about it. And once you learn to grasp and ingrain these concepts into your system, critical thinking will become second nature to you. For instance, seemingly *simple* decisions would not seem so simple anymore. Subsequently, you will push yourself to analyze every setting and scenario from different angles. Likewise, you would not merely jump at a particular opportunity out of sheer intuition. Through critical thinking, you will realize that there is actual weight to every choice you make, no matter how big or small. And that is a major concept that you should look to develop over time—understanding that your choices should not be taken for granted.

Embarking on this journey, there is a sense of optimism that you can greatly benefit from this book in ways you could never have imagined. Learning how to think critically is truly like having a superpower. It unlocks a part of yourself that you may not have known even existed in the first place. By learning to think critically, you are pushing the boundaries of what is possible. You can extract meaning, joy, and fulfillment from the seemingly mundane. Likewise, you could find depth and nuance in the ordinary. Hence, you would develop a greater appreciation for the beauty of everyday life. After all, critical thinking is about more than finding solutions to problems or coming up with innovative ideas. In fact, it is also about seeing the world through a lens allowing you to pick up on even the smallest details.

There are no limits to the profundity of learning. And when it comes to critical thinking, as you continue to grow and develop your cognitive abilities, so will your appreciation for learning. So, let us take this first step together as we embark on this immensely complex, deep, and wonderful world of advanced thought and reflection. Let us dive into the world of critical thinking.

Pillar 1:
Foundation

Foundations of critical thinking are a necessary building block for any successful thinker. They involve understanding the basics of the topic and being familiar with associated terms and models. Likewise, it includes analyzing problems using logical reasoning to make well-informed decisions. Considering alternative options is also vital in this process. However, the basic definitions are only a stepping stone to further understanding the practice. As such, more advanced skills can be acquired later to become an effective critical thinker truly.

Furthermore, knowledge, argument, inference, and evidence are integral to critical thinking. Knowledge is the information we can conclude. Then, arguments are attempts to convince someone of a given conclusion. Inferences are conclusions that can be logically drawn from given information. Meanwhile, evidence is factual information from which we can conclude. Each concept has a role in critical thinking. Ergo, you need to understand them to be an effective critical thinker.

Aside from general concepts, more specific models help critical thinkers in their reasoning. These models involve mapping out a problem and writing out the steps you can take to conclude. This can affect either immediate or root causes to help rectify issues in any situation. Likewise, these structured approaches help you as a critical thinker to stay on track. Plus, it ensures clarity of thought by eliminating false assumptions or irrelevant ideas that can muddle thinking.

To develop critical thinking skills, practicing it in various scenarios is essential. This could involve reading articles, engaging in critical discussions or debates, working on group projects, or conducting research. These tasks will help build and strengthen our critical thinking capacity and help form logical arguments.

Finally, it is essential to understand the concept of bias in critical thinking. When approaching a problem, it is crucial to remain objective and open-minded to find the best possible solution. This means that we should consider different perspectives. Also, we must stay impartial and maintain an awareness of preconceived notions that may impact their decision.

These elements, when taken together, form the foundations of critical thinking and are essential for being an effective critical thinker. As such, by understanding the various definitions and terms associated with critical thinking and the models and skills needed, we can effectively apply them, creating stronger, more informed decisions and conclusions.

Chapter 1:
Definition

When analyzing and evaluating information, our critical thinking works to arrive at a well-reasoned and unbiased conclusion. This cognitive process requires questioning assumptions, identifying biases, and examining evidence. Yet, to develop this skill, understanding the definition of critical thinking is the first step.

What Is Critical Thinking?

Critical thinking is an intellectual and reflective process of analyzing, evaluating, and synthesizing information from different sources to draw logical conclusions and solve problems. The purpose of critical thinking is to help people make better decisions, identify hidden implications, and recognize essential relationships *(Halpern, 2014)*. Likewise, it involves analyzing, synthesizing, and making judgments and decisions. Analysis involves identifying and breaking apart ideas and information into smaller components. Aside from that, you also examine how the parts relate to each other and the overall problem.

Subsequently, synthesis involves combining related information from different sources to form an argument or solution to the problem. Then, making judgments involves creating opinions or conclusions based on the analysis and synthesis of the data *(Halpern, 2014)*. Finally, decision-making determines the best course of action or solution to the problem based on the analysis, synthesis, and judgments made. These concepts seem overly complex or intimidating to you at first. But we can always break these ideas down later in the book so that they become more digestible.

Few abilities in the world rival critical thinking in terms of its importance. For example, a student was assigned a project to construct a bridge that could span across a river. Using her critical thinking skills, she realized that the essential part of the project was understanding the constraints of her materials and environment. To consider this, she developed a plan with factors such as the size of the river, how much weight the bridge would need to bear, and available materials in mind. Before presenting her completed project to her teacher, she tested it to ensure its structural integrity. In addition, she considered potential external impacts, such as strong winds or floods, that could affect its stability over time. With these considerations, she completed her project with excellent results.

Therefore, critical thinking is actively examining and evaluating information to solve problems and come to sound conclusions logically. It involves analyzing data, synthesizing information, making judgments, and forming decisions systematically.

Why Is Critical Thinking Important?

Critical thinking is more than just a problem-solving tool. As such, it also promotes critical and creative thinking, which encourages creativity in tackling complex problems. It allows us to think outside the box and consider innovative solutions that may have yet to be considered.

Moreover, it can help to create *"bigger picture"* perspectives when making decisions.

By taking a broader view of potential solutions, we can better evaluate their efficacy and how they impact all stakeholders involved. This includes considering the possible long-term benefits or consequences of any solution. Furthermore, considering the big picture enables us to devise strategies that can be beneficial in the long run. Plus, it allows us to create sustainable change in both personal and professional spheres.

Through critical thinking, we can develop an understanding that challenges pre-established beliefs, assumptions, values, and biases. In doing so, we open ourselves to diverse solutions that can be explored further before finally selecting a course of action. Ultimately, engaging in critical thinking before solving a problem helps us develop informed decisions and compelling solutions.

To be successful critical thinkers, we must analyze situations with an open mind. Taking a neutral stance and considering all possible options can help identify the best outcome for any problem. Additionally, looking beyond our biases allows for greater objectivity when making decisions.

The skills developed by exercising critical thinking can be applied in various situations. When it comes to making choices or formulating opinions on essential matters, these skills are invaluable. Engaging in this deliberate thought process ensures that our decisions are based on all the available facts. Likewise, it lets us adhere to good judgment rather than relying solely on intuition or snap judgment.

Moreover, critical thinking also has implications for communication with others. It is essential for interpreting messages accurately and making meaningful contributions to conversations. The ability to analyze arguments logically and draw logical conclusions from them is invaluable in making sure that differing perspectives are heard and understood correctly by everyone involved in a discussion.

Applying critical thinking to communication can help us better to understand another person's underlying goals and objectives. This can enable us to respond more effectively and create more meaningful conversations. Additionally, being aware of logical flaws, weak arguments, and illogical conclusions during a conversation can help us stay on the right track and achieve the desired outcomes.

Thinking critically can also give us the edge in any negotiation as we will be better prepared to spot discrepancies or inconsistencies in the other party's arguments. Furthermore, understanding the context of a conversation also allows us to establish a good rapport, which is essential for effective communication. Doing so creates an environment where constructive dialogue occurs and an open-minded approach is adopted.

Critical Thinking vs. Other Types of Thinking

As mentioned, critical thinking examines assertions and claims to draw logical conclusions based on evidence and facts. It is a systematic approach to analyzing and evaluating information from any source, including opinions and attitudes. Critical thinking involves the identification of assumptions, evaluation of arguments, application of standards for assessing the quality of evidence, identification of implications, and drawing logical conclusions. Furthermore, it enables us to use an evidence-based approach to problem-solving and decision-making.

Uncritical thinking, on the other hand, involves believing and accepting something without the application of critical thinking skills and without examining any evidence or facts. It is a way of believing without careful consideration or reasoning. Likewise, it relies on instinct, intuition, emotion, and personal preferences. Plus, it is often based on beliefs, prejudices, and biases. That said, it can lead to bias and decisions made without evaluation of evidence.

Like uncritical thinking, reactive thinking is a type of thinking in which we respond to a situation, typically without giving it much thought. Quick, unplanned decisions and emphasizing efficiency over accuracy characterize reactive thinking. Typically, it involves little to no evaluation of the evidence before deciding on a course of action. Besides that, it is heavily focused on the immediate needs of the situation. For instance, it is when we do not take the time to think deeply or objectively and instead rely on our previously held beliefs and assumptions. Likewise, no effort is made to contextualize the issue or problem, reflect on the implications or consequences of the decision, or consider alternative solutions.

Benefits of Critical Thinking in the Real World

Possessing the skill of critical thinking is integral to success in all areas of life, not only professional careers. This fact makes it even more vital to hone our critical thinking skills before entering a workplace. By utilizing this skill, we can break down issues, consider multiple solutions and their implications, and then make sound choices that benefit everyone involved. Moreover, critical thinking can help uncover innovative ways of approaching and solving problems when confronted with difficult situations.

Beyond that, critical thinking can further protect organizations from making risky decisions that could lead to losses. With well-developed critical thinking skills, we can identify potential risks quickly and efficiently while making decisions. As such, it allows us to make well-thought-out choices that prevent unnecessary expenses or other damages due to wrong conclusions.

Moreover, critical thinking is essential to succeed as a leader in our careers. When it comes to leading a team or organization, having the ability to think critically is necessary. For instance, critical thinking allows us to make informed, rational, and well-considered decisions. Furthermore, it will help us to take a step back and look at the bigger picture rather than making decisions based on emotions or personal bias. This skill also helps us identify potential problems before they arise and develop solutions for them. Thinking critically allows us to assess situations and develop the most effective solutions for our team or organization. This includes identifying potential risks, understanding the impact of our decisions, and effectively communicating our ideas to our team.

Aside from being effective in the workplace, critical thinking is essential for success in any educational setting. As we have discussed, it is the ability to look at a situation from different perspectives. Likewise, it weighs evidence and facts, evaluates information, and comes to an informed and reasoned conclusion. That said, critical thinking helps students understand a subject, identify inconsistencies and discrepancies in sources, and assess the relevance of information. Ergo encourages students to ask deeper questions and think beyond surface-level learning.

Subsequently, critical thinking is a valuable skill that can benefit students. For example, it can empower them to become more organized and focused in their academic work. Additionally, by honing their analytical skills, they can engage with course material on a deeper level and better remember what they have learned. Lastly, critical thinking can improve communication with peers and colleagues as they learn to articulate their ideas more effectively.

Moreover, critical thinking can help us understand different perspectives more and reduce our reliance on assumptions. By objectively evaluating multiple solutions to a problem, we are more likely to make informed decisions that will serve us well in the future. Similarly, by analyzing the pros and cons of available options, we can avoid any potential pitfalls associated with a particular choice.

Aside from that, critical thinking allows us to establish healthier relationships with those around us. By applying principles such as clear communication and respect for others' beliefs, we can create meaningful connections that last longer than superficial ones. As a result of using this skill set in social situations, conflicts are less likely to arise, and we can grow together rather than apart.

One way critical thinking can help us find success in our relationships is by promoting clear communication. Critical thinking involves examining our ideas, beliefs, and values with others. This helps foster a better understanding of our and other people's needs. Through this process of reflection, we can better understand and express our thoughts, feelings, and desires, leading to more meaningful conversations with others.

Another way critical thinking can help us find success in our relationships is by reducing conflict. When engaging in critical thinking, we actively explore how different perspectives and experiences can be mutually beneficial rather than seeing them as sources of disagreement or disputes. Thinking critically about relationships can help us identify areas of potential conflict and find ways to resolve them productively.

Ultimately, critical thinking can help us create healthy boundaries. As such, critical thinking allows us to understand both our own needs and the needs of others in a thoughtful, deliberate manner. This helps us gain insight into the appropriate and necessary boundaries in our relationships, leading to healthier and more fulfilling relationships.

Chapter 2:
Models

Advanced professionals in various industries recognize that critical thinking is paramount for success. Assessing information, considering the evidence, and making informed decisions or suggestions are crucial for any contemporary worker. Knowledge of different critical thinking models must be gained to hone this skill set best. Examples include proximate cause versus root cause, cognitive bias analysis, and Hanlon's Razor axiom. Studying and implementing those models can help develop our decision-making abilities considerably. Additionally, understanding basic statistics such as standard deviation and correlation can provide more helpful insight. As such, we can apply this wisdom when considering realistic outcomes and potential consequences while utilizing these models to make better conclusions.

Proximate and root-cause thinking are essential concepts in critical thinking as they enable us to think beyond the obvious surface-level explanations. Likewise, with them, we can identify the underlying causes of an issue. Root cause thinking, in particular, is a practical approach as it allows us to trace a problem back to its origin and develop an appropriate solution. Cognitive biases can also influence the quality of decisions. Therefore, it must be considered to reduce the chances of making an incorrect decision. Finally, Hanlon's Razor encourages us to imagine systems of cause and effect when confronted with unknown or complex issues.

Understanding and applying the models of critical thinking presented in this chapter will require a solid foundation in the principles and theories of critical thinking. Such principles include objectivity, logical reasoning, and arriving at conclusions. Hence, it is noteworthy to be familiar with the fundamental concepts and principles of critical thinking before engaging with the different models and their applications. Ultimately, this chapter provides a comprehensive overview of various critical thinking models and how each can maximize the quality of decisions.

Proximate vs. Root Cause

Proximate cause analysis is a valuable technique employed across fields like law enforcement, risk management, insurance, and engineering to determine the immediate cause of a specific event. The primary goal of this analysis is to identify the core issue behind the occurrence, enabling the development of strategies that address these foundational issues.

Beginning with examining the circumstances, this analysis illuminates the cause-and-effect relationship between the event and its potential triggers. Generally, the inquiry separates immediate causes—events directly preceding the incident—from contributing factors, which, while not directly responsible, played a part and indirectly influenced the outcome.

Once the preliminary queries are addressed, the process proceeds to evidence analysis to pinpoint potential causes. Typically, the analysis involves scrutinizing documents, photographs, witness statements, and other relevant materials to explain the event. The assessment should expose the most plausible cause, such as a design defect or human error.

Ultimately, the findings from the proximate cause analysis serve to formulate procedures and strategies that address the core issue, minimizing the chance of future occurrences. These strategies encompass process enhancements, employee training modifications, or operating procedure revisions.

Meanwhile, root cause analysis is an investigative method to discern and reduce the deep-seated issues behind a problem or incident. This technique generally includes a comprehensive analysis of the fundamental causes, facilitating the introduction of improved corrective and preventative measures. The overarching aim of this strategy is to gather information that illuminates potential points of failure encompassing processes, systems, machinery, and human factors.

A comprehensive consideration of all elements is essential to guarantee productive results in a root cause analysis. It should also involve investigating events and any external elements that could have affected the problem or incident. Tools such as surveys, interviews, historical document reviews, and evidence examinations are employed in this procedure.

After conducting these investigations, data-driven, actionable solutions should be identified to effect substantive changes addressing the root problems, thereby diminishing the chance of recurrence. In essence, root cause analysis can yield more dependable and efficient results for any problem or incident (Stafford, 2022).

When comparing proximate cause analysis and root cause analysis, both are problem-solving techniques aimed at identifying core issues and developing solutions. However, they diverge in the scope and depth of their approach. For instance, proximate cause analysis is a short-term problem-solving method. It emphasizes identifying the direct cause of a problem, focusing on the events preceding the issue but not deeply exploring the underlying contributing factors. Its primary objective is promptly identifying the most straightforward solution to the problem to prevent its future recurrence.

On the contrary, root cause analysis is a long-term problem-solving tool. It delves beyond the immediate cause of a problem, striving to identify all contributing factors. This investigative process aims to unearth the "root" of the problem for a thorough and complete resolution. Furthermore, root cause analysis endeavors to reveal any patterns or trends that may prevent future similar issues.

In summary, proximate and root cause analyses share many similarities but also possess distinct differences. Both techniques investigate and analyze a problem, considering its components and relationships. However, they diverge in the breadth and depth of their investigation. Proximate cause analysis focuses on the immediate cause, providing short-term solutions, whereas root cause analysis delves into the underlying contributing factors, offering comprehensive, long-term solutions.

Applying the Two Principles

A common example of proximate cause thinking can be found in a car owner's relationship with their vehicle. In a hypothetical car accident, a driver fails to come to a complete stop at a stop sign and crashes into a car already stopped at the intersection. Likely, a police officer might arrive at the accident scene and take it upon himself to determine which driver might have been at fault. Here is an example of what that police officer's thought process might be when using proximate cause analysis to assess the situation:

1. Gather evidence from the accident scene, such as witness statements or photographs.

2. Determine if any traffic laws or regulations were violated due to the crash.

3. Analyze all data collected to determine which party was primarily responsible for the accident.

4. Assess any mitigating circumstances that could affect liability, such as driver intoxication or road conditions.

5. Consider the physical injuries and property damage caused by the collision.

6. Evaluate all facts gathered to assess fault and liability.

7. Conclude whether one party should bear more responsibility than another for damages caused by the collision.

By merely assessing the situation, the police officer could determine which vehicle driver was at fault for the accident.

On the other hand, the root cause thinking methodology would take a different approach. As was mentioned, root cause thinking is a process used to investigate a problem by asking *"why"* several times until the actual cause is found. It can also be used to identify opportunities for improvement, prioritize solutions, and understand why a solution may not have worked in the past.

Imagine you are a student trying to understand why your grades suddenly dropped this semester. You can use root cause analysis to determine the underlying cause. First, you need to identify the symptoms that are causing the problem. In this case, the sign is your sudden drop in grades. Next, you need to look for potential underlying causes that could be causing this symptom. For example, *did you spend much less time studying or preparing for tests than the previous semester? Have you taken on more extracurricular activities or spent more time socializing?* Again, keep on asking yourself the question, *why*.

Once you have identified a few possible causes, you should investigate them further. For example, if you have taken on more extracurricular activities, *is there a way to reduce the time you spend on those activities without sacrificing your grades?* You can also look for any other potential causes impacting your grades. For instance, *has the difficulty of your classes changed compared to the previous semester? Is there an unexpected factor that has contributed to your drop in grades?* Finally, you can use all the information you have gathered to determine the root cause of the problem. Once you have identified the underlying cause, you can develop a plan of action to address it and get your grades back on track.

The benefits of knowing the distinctions between the two types of cause analysis are significant. Knowing the differences helps you better understand the contributing factors and conditions that led to an event or incident. From there, it will enable more informed decisions to prevent similar occurrences. In addition, it helps identify potential areas for improvement that can help prevent problems from happening again. Typically, you can use proximate cause thinking when identifying the immediate cause of an event, such as a workplace accident, medical malpractice, or a product failure. Likewise, you can use it to determine liability and establish preventative measures. Conversely, root cause analysis is ideal for investigating larger-scale issues such as industrial problems, process failures, and health and safety failures.

Cognitive Bias

A cognitive bias affects our decisions as an inherent feature of human nature. Often, we fail to assess a situation objectively, as their preconceived ideas and beliefs influence the way we interpret events and people. This can majorly impact decision-making, social behavior, perception, and evaluation of knowledge and information.

Cognitive biases are divided into two types: heuristics and biases. Heuristics are mental shortcuts used in decision-making. These heuristics can be divided into algorithmic *(automated decisions)* and heuristic *(based on rules of thumb)*. Meanwhile, biases are emotions or beliefs guiding our choices. Some common cognitive biases include confirmation bias, halo effect, status quo bias, availability heuristic, and fundamental attribution error. Other phenomena such as anchoring bias, representativeness heuristic and self-serving bias also play a role in human behavior.

For instance, a halo effect occurs when our pre-existing ideas about another person cause us to form an opinion based on incorrect assumptions rather than facts. Likewise, it is the tendency to make overly favorable assessments of a person or concept based on a single trait or characteristic. Then, the status quo bias is the disposition to pick the current state of affairs because it is familiar. Moreover, the availability heuristic is when we overestimate the probability of events we know or easily recall. Meanwhile, the fundamental attribution error is the bias to overestimate the role of one's internal dispositions. Yet, we underestimate the role of external factors in determining behavior.

Furthermore, fundamental attribution error happens when we attribute others' behavior to personal characteristics while overlooking external circumstances that could have affected the situation. Therefore, understanding different cognitive biases is essential for making informed decisions without relying on fallacies or prejudices.

Subsequently, when we make decisions based on information that reaffirms our existing beliefs and opinions, this is known as confirmation bias. As such, people exhibiting confirmation bias can be more likely to rely on emotional arguments rather than facts or evidence. This cognitive bias can lead to entrenched beliefs, making us less likely to consider opposing viewpoints and close ourselves off from new information.

For example, someone who believes in the death penalty may find research or anecdotal evidence confirming that it is an effective deterrent. Likewise, they will use such proofs to argue further its implementation instead of objectively considering the evidence for and against it. Due to this preference, their arguments can be unbalanced and lacking in accuracy. This sets them up to speak dismissively towards those who disagree with their views, reducing their ability to articulate valid arguments effectively. As a result, cognitive bias can lead to difficulty understanding the topic from all perspectives.

Moreover, this bias applies to moral and factual matters such as historical events or scientific theories. Confirmation bias frequently causes people to latch onto evidence that conforms to their preexisting beliefs. This limits how much we explore different angles on problems and encourages oversimplification of complex matters. Hence, we must look at information objectively rather than just accepting what is comfortable. Doing so allows us to better understand any situation's truth without skewing it with our preconceived notions.

Although cognitive biases often lead to inaccurate decisions, certain advantages can be gained from them. The availability heuristic allows for quick decision-making, the halo effect encourages positive behavior, and the status quo bias helps minimize potential risk. Likewise, even if it can be challenging to identify and counteract cognitive biases, we can use various techniques to reduce their influence. As such, we can consider other possibilities, looking at issues from an impartial viewpoint, gathering new data, and creating a process that is less prone to bias. By learning more about cognitive biases, we can make informed and confident choices while keeping our minds open to new possibilities.

Cognitive Bias in Decision-Making

Cognitive bias is an issue that can have a profound impact on decision-making. It involves us coming to erroneous conclusions due to limited or biased information. Often, these judgments are caused by personal interests, short-term gains, or preexisting perspectives.

One example of cognitive bias is the availability heuristic, which occurs when we make decisions based on easily accessible or memorable information. This can lead to focusing too heavily on specific pieces of evidence while overlooking other aspects of the decision-making process. For instance, news coverage of a particular scandal may sway our opinions without weighing all available evidence.

However, cognitive bias can be countered by diversifying sources and considering multiple points of view. Additionally, individual biases should be acknowledged and assessed so that decisions are made based on facts rather than emotions or beliefs. This way, we can ensure better outcomes for everyone involved.

Cognitive Bias in Memory

Cognitive bias can also affect memory in many ways, such as reconstructive memory, confirmation bias, hindsight bias, and availability heuristics *(Schmicking, 2014)*. The first type of cognitive bias, reconstructive memory, occurs when we fill in the gaps in our memories and create an inaccurate remembrance of the event. For example, if you are trying to remember a conversation you had with a friend last week, you may remember the conversation differently depending on your current emotions or beliefs. As such, when you feel outraged, you may recall that your friend said something rude, even though they may not have.

Besides that, cognitive bias impacts memory through confirmation bias, which occurs when we actively seek out information and memories that support our existing beliefs. For instance, if you strongly believe in a certain political party, you may remember more positive comments about that party when recounting conversations. Another example was the previously discussed example regarding one's stance on the death penalty.

Moreover, hindsight bias is the third cognitive bias affecting memory. This bias occurs when we are more likely to overestimate our ability to predict an outcome after it has happened *(Fischhoff, 2013)*. To illustrate, if you expected the outcome of a certain football match before it happened, you might be more likely to remember your prediction as accurate after it has happened.

Finally, the availability heuristic affects memory by altering how much we remember based on how easily we can access it *(Tversky & Kahneman, 1973)*. As such, if we have seen or heard news stories or statistics about a certain issue, we may be more likely to remember those things than those we have not been exposed to. Overall, cognitive bias significantly impacts memory, causing us to recognize stories and events based on their current values and beliefs and how easily we can access certain information.

Cognitive Bias in Perception

Aside from affecting memory, cognitive biases can impact perception. As such, it influences our information processing about our beliefs, expectations, and values. Due to that, we interpret and remember information differently than it occurred. This can lead to distorted memories, inaccurate impressions, and illogical decisions.

Under cognitive bias, confirmation bias affects our decisions, judgments, and behavior. It is the tendency to pay more attention to information that confirms our beliefs while disregarding evidence that contradicts them. For example, this bias is particularly apparent during elections. When faced with an election decision, people look for evidence that confirms their chosen candidate over any that would challenge their beliefs. Instead of objectively considering both sides of an argument before deciding, those displaying confirmation bias favor the side they already support. This can lead to an unbalanced opinion and a lack of understanding regarding why they may have taken a different stance. Yet, having an open mind is essential when forming opinions and engaging in political debates and any other discourse or decision-making process.

How Cognitive Bias Affects Everyday Life

Cognitive bias can be seen in almost every aspect of life, from the news we view to the language we use to our everyday interactions and relationships. In interpersonal relationships, cognitive bias can lead to misunderstanding and detract from the connection quality between two people. For instance, an individual may snap judgments about another based on their dress or appearance. This is an example of the halo effect, a cognitive bias in which one trait can affect a person's opinion of another. This often results in unwarranted assumptions and a lack of understanding, which can cause unnecessary misunderstandings and disconnects between individuals.

As mentioned, cognitive bias can lead to confirmation bias, a tendency to look at or interpret information in a way that confirms one's preconceived notions or beliefs. In relationships, this can lead to misunderstanding, as one or both parties may pay attention to information or events that only serve to confirm their existing beliefs, leading to further misunderstanding. For example, when two people disagree, they may focus on information that proves their point and deny or ignore any evidence that goes against their opinion.

Lastly, cognitive bias can negatively impact relationships when preconceived notions and stereotypes affect someone's perception of the other. This can create an environment of distrust and hatred and prevent a relationship from thriving and deepening. Prejudices and stereotypes are rooted in cognitive bias. While they may not be conscious, they can lead to misreading cues or ignoring important information or experiences that could bring the two people closer together.

Confirmation bias can also affect how an individual pursues learning and education. This bias is when we look for information, experiences, or sources that will reaffirm our beliefs and preconceptions. As such, we are more likely to accept information that aligns with our ideas. For instance, in a classroom environment, this bias can prevent students from assimilating new information and perspectives, as they are unconsciously more receptive to information confirming their worldview.

Another cognitive bias present in education is the anchoring effect. This is when one positional value or piece of information influences and affects the outcome of a decision or evaluation. In learning, an individual is likelier to use their reference point as the starting point for future estimations or judgments rather than considering external data or sources. This can lead to inaccurate conclusions and narrow-minded perspectives that impede further learning.

The availability heuristic is another cognitive issue that affects learning and education. People tend to overestimate the probability that an event that is more recent or easily recalled is more likely to happen in the future. This cognitive bias can be seen in learning processes when students are more drawn toward certain information than others based on its ease of recollection or current relevance.

Finally, the recency bias is when individuals give more weight to recent experiences than older experiences. This can be seen in education when a student is more likely to remember or apply information studied recently, as opposed to older material. This bias can lead to misallocating resources and an unequal focus on new information, resulting in shallow and underdeveloped long-term understanding and knowledge.

In conclusion, cognitive bias can be detrimental to everyday interactions and relationships. It can lead to misunderstanding, lack of connection, and distrust, preventing relationships from being as meaningful as possible. Likewise, it can stymy a person's growth regarding their overall learning and development. That said, we must become aware of our cognitive biases. Recognize how these biases may influence our perceptions and behaviors and try to look past these biases to connect with others more deeply.

Hanlon's Razor

Hanlon's Razor, a principle named after American physicist Robert J. Hanlon, guides our interpretation of others' actions. According to this philosophical razor, it is advisable not to attribute malicious intent to the behaviors of others when those actions can just as adequately be explained by carelessness or ignorance.

The purpose of Hanlon's Razor is to encourage us to practice humility and be more cautious in our judgment of others. Doing so enables us to look beyond the surface level to be more open to better understanding others. Plus, it suggests that we should be willing to give others the benefit of the doubt when misunderstandings arise, as this is often a better approach than immediately assuming malicious intent.

Moreover, Hanlon's Razor has been lauded for its potential to reduce misunderstandings and conflicts. Likewise, it is known for its ability to encourage individuals to think critically about their assumptions. Besides that, it is a reminder that we should not be too judgmental when it comes to interpreting the actions of others, as many complications can stem from the assumption of malintent. Such principles can help us maintain strong relationships interpersonally and in the workplace.

A Brief Historical Perspective

The philosophy of skepticism and suspicion has been used for centuries to navigate difficult situations in engineering, science, business, and politics. It advises one against jumping to conclusions prematurely or attributing a problem to more nefarious causes when simpler explanations are available. This concept was first cited in works from the 19th century, but it was popularized more recently by Patrick F. McManus' 1980s article.

Following its publication, Hanlon's Razor spread widely throughout magazines, journals, books, and academic papers. Nowadays, it is an established part of the lexicon as a wise proverb and a trusted reminder of balanced decision-making when dealing with complex issues. It can also reflect McManus' skeptical views that it is unwise to disparage any phenomenon until we understand its root cause.

How Hanlon's Razor Is Applied

Hanlon's Razor is an adage that can be applied to many facets of life. This principle encourages us to assume the best of others rather than assume the worst and assume that bad outcomes are solely because of malicious intent. This is particularly beneficial in interpersonal relationships and conflict resolution, as it can help us to remain open-minded and see things from different perspectives.

Here is an example of how Hanlon's Razor can manifest in the workplace. Imagine that in a hypothetical office setting, whenever there is conflict, there is a tendency for managers often to attribute the mistakes of subordinates to malicious intent and subsequently take corrective action against the subordinate. However, when the managers applied Hanlon's Razor and tried to understand the reasons behind their subordinate's mistakes, they could recognize the situation more objectively and attempt to resolve the problem without punishing the subordinate, which usually leads to a better outcome.

The application of Hanlon's Razor can be beneficial in various contexts. It encourages us to be more generous to people and assume that a situation might be more complex. Likewise, it urges respectful conversations and more balanced approaches to problem-solving.

In pop culture, Hanlon's Razor is often used in movies or television shows as a plot device to show how characters can be wrong about the intentions of another character or person. For example, in the film Shrek, the titular character is tasked with fulfilling the order of the film's villain as compensation for saving his home. He is lumped together with the Donkey character, whom he treats terribly throughout the time they are together on their quest. With compassionate understanding, Donkey realizes that Shrek is not being deliberately malicious. Instead, he is focused on what he believes is the only way to save his home. This is Hanlon's Razor, where Donkey can look past Shrek's behavior and understand that his intentions are ultimately honorable.

Common Criticisms of the Razor

While Hanlon's Razor is more positive in tone and disposition, it is not a principle without its fair share of detractors. Common criticisms of Hanlon's Razor must be considered when applying it.

Firstly, Hanlon's Razor has been criticized for being too simplistic. As such, it implies that all negative actions can be explained by sheer ignorance rather than intentional wrongdoing. While it is true that intent is often unknowable and that incorrect assumptions can lead to serious repercussions, Hanlon's Razor can be used to excuse those whose intentions are truly malicious. In essence, it reduces the emphasis and consequence placed on negative behavior that might be intentional.

Secondly, Hanlon's Razor can be applied without considering the experience of those wronged. Thus, it denies them agency and acknowledgment of their experiences. This can manifest itself in an attempt by people to discredit an individual's experience in favor of more benign reasoning, which can cause further harm in the process.

Finally, Hanlon's Razor can be misused when applied hastily without considering the context or the situation. For example, if a person has been the victim of multiple destructive events, attributing it to mere stupidity or lack of competence can minimize their experience and provide an excuse for the behavior (Rifkin, 2017).

In conclusion, although Hanlon's Razor can help determine a motive and understand a situation, it is crucial to be mindful of its criticisms to ensure that it is applied appropriately and fairly.

Chapter 3:
Skills Needed

Critical thinking is a skill developed over time, and it has several sub-skills that need to be developed for it to be effective. These include problem-solving, decision-making, effective communication, creativity, and reasoning. Problem-solving involves the ability to identify, analyze and solve complex problems. Then, decision-making requires weighing various options and determining the best course of action. Furthermore, effective communication involves communicating ideas and thoughts to others using clear and concise language. Meanwhile, creativity consists of thinking outside the box to develop innovative solutions to problems. Likewise, reasoning involves being able to analyze an argument or claim to make a sound judgment.

For critical thinking to be effective, all these sub-skills must be developed and utilized. Developing these skills will enable you to make better decisions, develop creative solutions and better understand complex situations. This chapter provides an overview of the essential skills needed for critical thinking. We will discuss how observation, analysis, interpretation, inference, evaluation, communication, and problem-solving are necessary for developing a more critical approach to any subject matter. Also, we will explore how these skills can be developed and strengthened to become more effective thinkers. In addition, we will discuss the role of emotions and feelings in thinking critically and the advantages of learning to think critically. By the end of this chapter, you should better understand the vital skills needed for critical thinking and how these can be applied.

Observation

Observation is carefully watching, noting, and recording what is seen, heard, or experienced. As such, observing and recognizing patterns, identifying causes, and recognizing connections are all necessary skills for critical thinking. Through careful observation, we can identify trends in data, evaluate evidence, and draw informed conclusions. Aside from that, observations not only help to gain insight and better understanding. Yet, it can also provide feedback for modifications or changes.

Moreover, with this skill, you can analyze a situation and conclude. Likewise, it can identify potential opportunities and strategies that can be used to address current circumstances. Through careful observation, we can identify underlying causes and suggest solutions or approaches that could lead to lasting results. This ability to observe is also widely expressed in the field of medicine, engineering, and other scientific endeavors. Plus, observation is essential for creativity and problem-solving. By identifying patterns, causes, and relationships, we better understand the problem or situation and can develop creative solutions. It also provides insight into thinking and approaching a problem, which helps spark innovative solutions.

An example of how observation is practiced in critical thinking is by doing a root cause analysis. In a root cause analysis, a problem is observed. After that, it will be broken down into smaller components to identify the root cause. This helps to understand the underlying factors that led to the problem. By breaking down a problem and observing each component, we can better understand what is causing an issue and create strategies for problem-solving. For instance, if a student is struggling in school, their grades can be observed to identify any problems potentially. This information can then be broken down further to observe whether any specific subjects are complicated or if there are other factors at play. By doing this, a strategy can then be created to help the student overcome their difficulties.

Another scenario wherein observation can be crucial in critical thinking is in the workplace context. Imagine that your team is in charge of trying to devise a plan to reduce energy usage at an office building; observation is critical to success. By closely evaluating the building's occupants and practices, you can identify where energy is wasted and develop a tailored plan to address those issues. Lastly, you can use effective observation to identify and implement strategies to reduce energy costs and environmental impact.

Analysis

The analysis involves breaking down complex problems into smaller, more manageable parts or determining the relationships between different pieces of information. This can help us better understand the problem or situation and identify potential solutions or strategies. Through analysis, we can also recognize patterns, draw connections, and make informed decisions.

Likewise, analysis allows us to evaluate information objectively. This involves analyzing the strengths and weaknesses of different perspectives and assessing their logical connections. When done effectively, analysis can help individuals identify whether an argument is valid or invalid. It can also determine the accuracy of information. Furthermore, this skill is essential for researching and understanding complex topics.

For example, you are presented with the problem of solving a conflict between two departments in a company. To solve this problem, break down the problem into its parts. This would involve looking at each department in detail and analyzing the sources of the conflict. Then, assess the evidence by looking at the different perspectives of each department and understanding their goals and motivations. Lastly, evaluate the possible solutions, weighing the pros and cons of each option before making a decision.

Overall, analysis is a crucial skill for critical thinking as it encourages individuals to evaluate information objectively, draw logical connections, and consider multiple perspectives before concluding. By honing this skill, we can become better problem solvers and make more informed decisions.

Interpretation

Interpretation is an essential part of critical thinking that involves analyzing data and information to gain insight into a subject. Besides that, it is a cognitive process involved in understanding an individual's subjective opinion or viewpoint. It consists in breaking down the meaning of a text or expression using logic, reason, and prior knowledge. An individual engaged in interpretation can understand complex ideas, identify the main elements of a message, analyze relationships between concepts, and make assumptions about various implications. This process is often used in critical thinking to evaluate facts and evidence gathered to draw a logical conclusion that can be used to make a decision or solve a problem.

An example of how the skill of interpretation is practiced in critical thinking can be seen in the scientific method. Scientifically, hypotheses are formulated, experiments are designed to test the ideas, data is collected, and then conclusions are drawn based on the results of the experiments. By interpreting the results, a scientist can gain insight into the validity of the hypothesis and conclude the data that can be used to form a different theory. Additionally, scientists must be able to interpret the results of other researchers' experiments to build upon their existing knowledge. Ultimately, practicing interpretation in critical thinking enables us to understand the world around us better.

In developing interpretation skills, critical thinkers should be able to identify and analyze key aspects of the information they are looking at. This involves focusing on the main ideas and arguments presented in the source material and understanding the context of the material. It also means analyzing the logic of the discussion and looking for any inconsistencies that may be prevalent.

Inference

Inference is a critical thinking skill that involves deriving conclusions without direct evidence, relying instead on patterns of thought and understanding. It is also the process of concluding information and evidence known or assumed to be true. This skill requires logical reasoning and prior knowledge of universal concepts such as cause and effect, similarity, and contradiction to interpret and analyze data. Similarly, it is a crucial part of critical thinking because it helps to interpret and understand complex situations, relationships, and ideas with limited information or usable data.

To enhance inference skills, it is necessary to practice in various contexts. Exercises such as making inferences from news articles, interpreting figures and graphs, analyzing written texts, and making connections between ideas can all be used to develop inference skills. It is also noteworthy to actively monitor your thinking, mainly when concluding. This can be done by asking oneself questions such as: *How did I reach this conclusion? What evidence supports my conclusion? Is there any contrary evidence that I should consider?*

Evaluation

Evaluation is a critical thinking skill that requires assessing and appraising facts, opinions, beliefs, or arguments. It requires us to judge the information's merit, accuracy, and appropriateness. This is often done by synthesizing multiple pieces of evidence or analyzing the logic to support a conclusion.

For example, look at the evidence presented when evaluating an argument. *Is it relevant? Is the evidence from reliable sources? Are the conclusions logical and consistent?* Once the evidence has been examined, we need to consider the context of the argument. *Is the context relevant, or does it have any implications for the argument?*

Developing evaluation skills requires a detailed and thoughtful approach. First, we should understand the context of the evaluated information and become familiar with the presented arguments. This involves carefully reading, analyzing, and summarizing materials. Applying evaluation strategies, such as point-counterpoint or claims-evidence-reasoning, can help in understanding the details of the structure and arguments being presented.

Once the information has been analyzed and summarized, develop evaluation criteria to understand the presented evidence's merits. This means carefully examining claims, counterpoints, evidence, and reasoning presented to assess how relevant, complete, and accurate they are. It is also important to determine whether there is bias in the information and ensure the sources used are reliable and credible.

The last step in the evaluation process is to synthesize the material. Then, reach an informed opinion about the material being evaluated. As such, it involves considering the soundness of the argument, the accuracy of the evidence, the logical connections of the reasoning, and the importance of the conclusion.

These steps provide a framework for developing the evaluation skill, though we should continue to refine our strategies as they become more comfortable with the process. With practice, we can build evaluation skills to the fullest potential, essential for practicing critical thinking.

Communication

Communication is a skill that allows for the free exchange of ideas. Moreover, it is the ability to put forward well-reasoned arguments supporting a position or point of view. This skill is vital for critical thinking because it allows for exploring different perspectives and considering further facts and evidence. To be an influential critical thinker, it is essential to communicate ideas and opinions to others effectively. Effective communication involves being able to explain your ideas clearly and concisely. Other than that, it means being able to listen to and consider the opinions of others.

When deciding on a team project, effective communication ensures that everyone understands the proposed plan and all the relevant information being discussed. All team members must be able to express their thoughts and ideas, as well as listen and respond to the ideas of others. This requires active and open communication to decide based on understanding, agreement, and respect. The use of communication is vital for any successful critical thinking process.

Consider when you feel like you have some great ideas and innovative breakthroughs. You need to communicate these ideas clearly and effectively to your peers, colleagues, and supervisor to receive feedback and consider all aspects of your idea. In such situations, effective communication allows your ideas to be understood, and people can assess their merits accurately. However, remember that ideas are only as good as one's ability to communicate them to others. Your great idea will mean nothing to someone else if you cannot express it to them in a way they can understand or appreciate.

Sharpening the skill of communication can help improve your critical thinking capabilities. A few ways to develop this skill include actively listening to others, considering different perspectives, and focusing on clarity and logic in communication. It is also essential to consider the audience when communicating to ensure the message is well-received. Reading extensively and engaging in debates and discussions can also improve communication skills.

The 4 Pillars of Critical Thinking

Problem-Solving

Problem-solving is a critical thinking skill that involves identifying and defining problems. Likewise, it allows us to generate potential solutions, evaluate and select the most effective solution, and implement it. It is an essential life skill that should be developed and practiced to improve our ability to solve problems promptly and effectively.

Various methods and techniques can be used to develop the skill of problem-solving. The most common techniques are trial and error, brainstorming, and the systematic approach. Through trial and error, we can try different solutions and observe their effects before deciding. Brainstorming encourages creative thinking to identify potential solutions that could be useful. Then, the systematic approach involves breaking down the problem into smaller parts. After that, we determine the cause and its effects and devise solutions to the problem. Other methods, such as the analytical problem-solving approach, can also be used.

Pillar 2:
Process

The process of critical thinking involves a structured approach to evaluating and analyzing information. Through this systematic approach, snap judgments and faulty reasoning can be avoided. It also helps identify biases, assumptions, and fallacies in arguments that might lead to wrong conclusions or flawed decisions.

Not only does the critical thinking process provide ideal outputs. Yet, it also supports creative problem-solving by exploring the same issue from various angles. Seeking different opinions and resources from amateur and expert sources can bring new insights and give a more balanced view of the situation.

However, all these steps are not just beneficial for improving decision-making. As such, they are also crucial for enhancing communication skills with the help of critical thinking. Using strong evidence and logical arguments helps generate lively conversations about relevant topics and encourages thoughtful participation in debates.

Exploring different ideas, debating with others, and questioning our beliefs is essential to developing critical thinking skills. Such practices promote creativity and encourage the formation of sound conclusions based on facts, data, and research. It also takes place over time, allowing us to assess our thought processes, reflect upon open-ended questions, and challenge existing assumptions and biases. Likewise, it lets us evaluate the information for relevance and accuracy before making an appropriate decision or resolution.

Beyond identifying problems, conducting research, and analyzing arguments, there are other elements to consider when engaging in critical thinking. This includes understanding the subject matter context and knowledge. Aside from that, we need to recognize potential sources of bias that could influence decisions. Social intelligence is also vital to develop empathy and perspective when communicating with others or engaging in team projects.

With these ideas taken into account, it becomes easier to appreciate how important the practice of critical thinking is when forming judgments around any given subject. As such, this pillar will cover all the necessary critical thinking processes.

Chapter 4:
Identify the Problem or Issue

The first step in the critical thinking process is to identify the problem. This involves closely examining the facts, conditions, and situations that gave rise to the problem and exploring the various possible causes.

To accurately identify and diagnose the problem, it is usually necessary to use a systematic approach. First, it is crucial to gather and analyze as much information as possible and analyze it. This might include interviews with the parties involved, investigations, surveys, or other data-gathering methods. The gathered data can frame the problem by defining the facts and exploring potential causes. Ultimately, you should be looking to answer the question: *What is happening?*

Next, consider the consequences of the problem and ask "why" questions to get to the issue's root. Ideas and perspectives from many stakeholders should be incorporated into the process to form a comprehensive view of the situation. Brainstorming sessions, with all relevant stakeholders present, can benefit this process. So, from asking *'what is happening,'* you are now in the process of asking *'why is this happening?'*

Finally, the problem solving should be concretely defined with measurable objectives that can be evaluated. This involves looking at the data and synthesizing the information to understand how the problem might be solved. From asking those preliminary questions, you can draw certain assumptions and theories about the situation and the many nuances that make it up. You might even have a few assumptions about how you can approach solving the problem.

If you need more help, here are a few other questions you can look to ask yourself during this phase of the process:

- **What is the issue or problem?** This question can help narrow down the focus and clarify the problem. It helps provide context to understand the full complexity of the situation.

- **What caused this problem?** Understanding the cause of a problem can provide insight into possible solutions and helps to identify any underlying issues affecting the situation.

- **What are the consequences of this problem?** Identifying the implications of a problem can help focus on the magnitude of the issue and help prioritize the need for addressing it.

- **Who is affected by the problem?** Understanding who is affected by the problem can help identify potential stakeholders, which can help to inform the solution-building process.

- **Are there any barriers that could prevent a solution from being successful?** Identifying any potential barriers can help to inform any changes that need to be made or strategies that need to be implemented to ensure the success of any solutions.

- **What resources are needed to solve the problem?** Identifying the resources required to solve the problem can help ensure that the available resources are used effectively and efficiently.

- **What are the alternatives or options to solve the problem?** Thinking through the different choices or options to solve the problem can help to create a comprehensive list to consider when deciding on the best solution.

Chapter 5:
Research, Opinions, and Arguments

Research and data-gathering are essential parts of the critical thinking process. It involves identifying sources of information, collecting and organizing data, and analyzing and synthesizing it to conclude. Specifically, research involves assembling evidence from a variety of sources to understand the topic or problem at hand fully. As such, it is essential to identify reliable sources of information that can provide accurate and thorough data to work with. This includes primary and secondary sources such as books, articles, interviews, surveys, and other quantitative or qualitative data.

Meanwhile, data-gathering is collecting, organizing, and analyzing the information. The data is organized in a way that makes sense and is easily accessible for further analysis. This involves categorizing and summarizing the information or data points and determining their relationships. Then, analysis is conducted on the data gathered and organized. A critical thinker will look at the data and use it to determine patterns, identify trends, and draw logical conclusions. They will evaluate the data and draw inferences and insights to understand the problem or issue better.

However, before we get to that phase, we must continue to sharpen our ability to gather relevant data and information. This step is essential in the critical thinking process. It enables the critical thinker to thoroughly understand an issue or topic and draw conclusions based on their analysis. With this knowledge, we can make better decisions, develop more effective solutions, and think more strategically.

The Kinds of Sources

When performing research and data gathering, the quality of sources is crucial. Quality sources are reliable, have appropriate information, and provide an appropriate and well-researched conclusion. Further, sources should have a degree of objectivity and accuracy *(Mandalios, 2013)*.

Quality sources are essential since they provide us with accurate and objective findings. A research question can be answered accurately only when a quality source of evidence is used. Yet, the research and data-gathering findings may be inaccurate without a quality source. As a result, any conclusions and decision-making based on such findings could be erroneous and far from the real outcomes.

Also, quality sources help to ensure that only relevant and current information is used in the research and data-gathering process. With such a source, the researcher can use up-to-date and well-researched information in their analysis. This is beneficial as conclusions from the research and data-gathering process can be more comprehensive and accurate.

Finally, quality sources give researchers greater confidence in their findings. If a source is of low quality, the researcher may be unable to draw accurate or useful conclusions from the data gathered. On the other hand, a quality source can help to reduce any uncertainties regarding the reliability of the research and data-gathering results.

Sources can also be categorized into two different groups: *primary and secondary sources.* Primary sources in research are direct records of past events or phenomena that a direct participant or observer generated during the events or phenomena. Examples of primary sources include diaries, interviews, original records, artifacts, photographs, and works or writings of the period. They can also have the results of scientific experiments, studies, surveys, and pools. Likewise, they provide an immediate first-hand view of a topic and allow researchers to gauge the factual accuracy of the information.

The qualities and traits of primary sources in research are originality, authenticity, and directness, as they contain firsthand accounts of the events or phenomena they document. These sources provide insight into the original events and make it possible to reconstruct their context. Primary sources often challenge existing interpretations as they offer access to first-hand accounts of what happened.

On the other hand, secondary sources in research are interpretations and analyses based on primary sources. Examples of secondary sources include books, journal articles, documentaries, reviews, commentaries, encyclopedias, and websites. Secondary sources allow researchers to understand a topic more comprehensively by providing critical analysis, interpretation, and summarization of the original primary sources.

Moreover, secondary sources in research are those that offer context, analysis, and interpretation. They provide a higher-level perspective on the events or phenomena and allow researchers to gain a comprehensive overview of the topic. These sources often provide detailed critical analyses and interpretations of the original primary sources.

To sum it up, primary sources and secondary sources differ from one another in the level of detail that they provide. Primary sources provide firsthand accounts of the events or phenomena and are often more detailed and provide more specific information than secondary sources. Conversely, secondary sources provide a broader, higher-level perspective on the topic and provide more analytical and interpretive information than primary sources.

Evaluating the Quality of Sources

Conducting research and evaluating the quality of sources requires critical thinking. When assessing data quality, reliability and relevance must always be considered. To assess the reliability of a source, examine its peer-review status, accuracy level, information completeness, and recency. Relevancy is just as crucial as it entails considering if the source is current. Also, it ensures a comprehensive listing of references and if an expert in the field wrote it.

In addition to assessing reliability and relevance, the currency is also indispensable when evaluating the quality of sources. Currency means that the source must be up-to-date with new developments in its topic. As such, older research may not reflect current professional opinions or modern best practices. Transparency is also vital since reliable sources should reveal their authorship clearly and provide contact information for inquiries. Understanding these sources' relevance and reliability helps better understand their topics and make informed decisions.

The 4 Pillars of Critical Thinking

There are so many questions that you can ask yourself when judging a particular piece of data based on its source, such as:

- Is the information current and relevant to the research topic?

- Is it fact-based and authoritative, or is it opinion-based conjecture?

- Do ample evidence and credible sources support the facts, or is the evidence incomplete or unconvincing?

- Does the source offer a balanced viewpoint with much supporting evidence, or does it take a one-sided approach?

Aside from these two traits, investigate other factors, such as the accuracy and completeness of the information. Likewise, check whether the source is a peer-reviewed document published by an authoritative source. Sources such as books, peer-reviewed journal articles, authoritative websites, and subject experts are generally more reliable than popular news sources, blogs, or social media.

Chapter 6:
Analyze the Arguments

Argumentation is essential to critical thinking and involves identifying, analyzing, and evaluating evidence. It requires us to construct sound and persuasive arguments to reach a conclusion about a certain claim or proposition. Through this process, debaters can draw reliable conclusions that lead to informed decisions.

Moreover, arguments can come in multiple forms, such as written or verbal debates, conversations, research presentations, and academic writing. Knowing how to make compelling arguments relies on gathering evidence, reasoning logically, and critically evaluating the validity of claims. Using well-thought-out prose can further emphasize a point or opinion and make it more convincing.

In addition to forming arguments based on reliable evidence to support an idea or perspective, critical thinking extends beyond the argumentation's scope. It includes recognizing biases and assumptions made while conducting fact-finding research. Besides that, it developed creative solutions for complex problems with unbiased judgment through careful reasoning and synthesis of data or facts.

The Structure of Arguments

Arguments are constructed to support or refute a point and can be created in several ways. A premise is an accepted claim or assumption that serves as the argument's starting point. This could then be used to build towards a conclusion or else to prove another premise. The validity of an argument's conclusion relies on the accuracy and strength of its premises. When these are incorrect, then the overall result will suffer too.

To evaluate an argument effectively, all relevant evidence must be considered. This includes the premise(s), how it supports the conclusion and the connection between them. If there is any disparity between what is presented as evidence and its relevance to the argument's conclusion, it should raise questions about its reliability. Credibility and source authority should also be considered when assessing arguments.

Using examples can provide clarity and context within arguments relying only on abstract concepts. For instance, in proving why something was true or false based on facts, providing a specific situation that illustrates those facts may help better visualize the concept being discussed. Furthermore, connecting this example back to the original topic may further emphasize the claims made by the argumentation presented.

However, arguments must remain logical throughout for them to stand up against skeptical scrutiny. As such, it requires each step in a discussion to lead inevitably up to its outcome. When evaluating an argument, concentration should focus on reaching one predetermined end. Then, think critically about every claim made to arrive at a valid conclusion from sound premises. Any assumptions made along the way must remain logically consistent.

On the other hand, if the premises of an argument are not accepted, then the conclusion will not be valid. For instance, conclusions are the endpoint of an argument and are typically a conclusion or solution to a problem. In other words, conclusions result from the logical progression of arguments.

Hence, the structure of an argument usually consists of premises, evidence, and a conclusion. The premise or premises provide the evidence the author needs to make a conclusion or solution. Then, the conclusion is the logical result of the premise or premises and the evidence. Premises and conclusions, when combined, form a valid argument.

Arguments vs. Non-Arguments

Previously, we learned that an argument is a type of reasoning in which the conclusion is drawn from one or more premises. The premises provide supporting evidence for the conclusion and typically involve some form of logical reasoning. A non-argument, by contrast, does not involve any form of logical reasoning. However, it may include observations, facts, opinions, or questions that do not lead to a conclusion.

Arguments, therefore, are statements that contain both premises and conclusions. They do not require that one have any expertise in argumentation; it is simply necessary to have a logical understanding of how premises can lead to conclusions. The conclusion of an argument should be consistent with the premises. When the premises themselves are sound, they should also be logically valid. Further, arguments should always contain evidence-based premises. For example, an argument claiming that the Earth is round would include evidence-based premises, such as scientific measurements or observations from orbiting satellites.

Non-arguments, on the other hand, do not contain evidence-based premises. Thus, they do not necessarily lead to any specific conclusion. Instead, non-arguments generally consist of observations, facts, opinions, or questions. For example, an observation that it is snowing outside does not necessarily lead to any conclusion and could be considered a non-argument. Similarly, questions such as *"why is the sky blue?"* do not lead to a conclusion and are thus non-arguments. Furthermore, opinion like chocolate is better than vanilla do not necessarily require evidence-based premises. Ergo, this statement is considered a non-argument.

Banking on what we learned earlier, the presence of a premise and a conclusion indicate the formation of an argument. Any sentiment devoid of these two things may, more often than not, be classified as a non-argument. Arguments require a logical understanding of how premises can lead to conclusions, while non-arguments generally do not.

Chapter 7:
Identify Assumptions and Biases

In this chapter, we will discuss what an underrated and often-overlooked aspect of critical thinking is. Not many people realize that one of the most important steps related to critical thinking is identifying assumptions and challenging biases. This involves recognizing possible faulty reasoning and identifying the underlying assumptions and biases that may be present in a thought process.

To identify assumptions and challenge biases in critical thinking, we should actively question our thought processes and the decisions and opinions of others. Likewise, we should consider different points of view, pay attention to complex nuances, and examine underlying assumptions. More importantly, we should recognize our biases and the biases of others and look for alternate interpretations or explanations. Research or evidence should be sought to support or refute claims and ideas *(Mavrodes, 2019)*. When we can find reputable research or evidence to support our claims, then it takes biases out of the equation. For now, we will learn all about assumptions and biases, where they are most commonly found, and how we can avoid them in the process of critical thinking.

Defining Assumptions and Biases

Assumptions are the unstated preconditions present in an argument or an idea. They are not necessarily true but provide the basis for certain conclusions. For example, an assumption may be made that all people who wear glasses have poor vision. This assumption is inaccurate and reflects a bias, which can be challenged.

Biases are particular beliefs, values, or judgments that can lead to distorted thinking. They can be implicit or explicit, conscious or unconscious, influencing our conclusions and opinions. For example, a person may be biased towards a particular type of person or group because of their existing beliefs.

Assumptions and bias in the process of critical thinking refer to the beliefs, expectations, and theories again which we draw conclusions without a logical basis. We subconsciously base our opinions on pre-existing values, attitudes, or experiences, and these assumptions can completely change the outcome of our thought processes. Assumptions and biases are a natural part of the thought process, so it is vital to be aware of them to make an informed decision.

There are many ways through which assumptions and biases can pop up during the process of analyzing a particular problem or issue:

- **Presumption.** Assuming all potential outcomes to be true before fully exploring all the alternatives.
- **Ostracism.** Ignoring evidence or opposing viewpoints that do not agree with one's own opinion.
- **Cherry-picking.** Only selecting supporting information and disregarding contradictory facts that may disprove an idea or conclusion.

- **Personal experience.** Relying heavily on our experiences to make decisions without considering other viable options.

- **Subjectivity.** Giving more weight to anecdotal stories, rumors, or beliefs than scientific research.

Common Areas of Bias

Bias can manifest in a multitude of ways, from the way we perceive others to how we learn and make decisions. Confirmation bias, for example, is when an individual focuses on information that reinforces their beliefs and disregards evidence that contradicts them. Priming bias is another form of bias in which past experiences influence one's initial response to a stimulus.

The implications of such biases are far-reaching. As such, it can lead to poor decision-making or clouded thinking by prompting individuals to look at an issue through just one perspective or be swayed by preconceived notions. People may also start accepting information without consideration or rejecting facts opposing their worldviews.

Besides causing blinkered judgment, bias also opens the door for spreading misinformation as those with certain opinions tend to share only select types of information. To prevent such circumstances, individuals need to recognize their biases and strive for objectivity by seeking out different points of view and critically assessing the available evidence. Awareness of common areas of bias can also aid greatly in this regard, as it helps recognize when preconceived notions might be getting in the way.

Cultural

Cultural bias can have wide-reaching consequences, from creating false expectations of certain groups to fostering discrimination and prejudice. In the U.S., Asian Americans have often been reduced to the *"model minority"* stereotype, based primarily on their hard work and outward success. This oversimplified view of achievement disregards the numerous inequities many in this group face, such as language barriers, poverty, limited access to education and healthcare, and an increased risk of hate crimes.

In addition to these challenges, stereotypes like the *"model minority"* perpetuate a sense of false competition between diverse cultural communities. By placing some cultures higher on an imaginary pedestal than others over superficial attributes like success or appearance, those who do not fit preconceived notions are subject to scorn and ridicule.

To combat this cycle of stereotyping and marginalization, we must embrace a more inclusive definition of what it means to succeed in our society. Aside from that, based on empathy and understanding of cultural differences rather than unfair generalizations. By reevaluating our expectations of each other through honest dialogue and meaningful action, we can make real progress toward establishing a more equitable world where everyone is seen for their merits rather than simplistic labels.

Overall, it is crucial to recognize the potential for negative and unfair cultural biases to exist. Unconscious (or conscious) biases can harm cultural and religious groups and lead to discrimination, prejudice, and other forms of marginalization. Therefore, it is essential to treat all people with respect and take the time to learn about another individual's culture, background, and values.

Religious

Prejudice based on faith can be seen in a multitude of ways. Apart from the common examples, like being denied employment or excluded from social activities due to one's beliefs, individuals may also experience covert forms of discrimination. This can include subtle gestures such as pointing out someone's religious differences or unequally distributing resources between those of different faiths.

In some cases, religious bias is taken to violent extremes. This includes physical and verbal aggression towards those not following the same religion or beliefs. Moreover, it includes vandalism and damage done to places of worship with minority beliefs. In extreme cases, this can even lead to genocide and mass killings based on faith.

The consequences of religious bias are far-reaching and can have long-term effects on the person experiencing prejudice and their communities. Discrimination leads to feelings of isolation, marginalization, hurt, anger, and fear, which can harm relationships with family members or people from the same faith group. It hinders an individual's professional growth while impacting their mental health and self-esteem.

Aside from that, an example of a subtle yet impactful religious bias is how people with certain religious backgrounds are portrayed in the media. A 2014 report released by the Council on American-Islamic Relations (CAIR) concluded that Muslims who appeared on news channels were overwhelmingly depicted as *"villains, terrorists, or persons of security interest."* This portrayal and the idea that Muslims are to blame for some of the world's most heinous terror atrocities perpetuated an atmosphere of fear and mistrust toward this traditionally marginalized community.

Therefore, religious bias has long been a part of our society, both in the past and present, and can be based on any form of personal religious beliefs. However, it is important to recognize and work to eliminate religious bias and destructiveness to create a more inclusive and equitable society.

Racial

Biases based on skin color, ethnicity, and cultural identity occur when people make assumptions or come to conclusions about an individual or group because of their racial identity. These biases can lead to unfairness in treatment and situations of disadvantage. Moreover, they are often rooted in historical power dynamics that cause members of minority groups to be excluded and even delegitimized.

At the same time, racism has far-reaching effects beyond individuals. Studies have demonstrated that unequal opportunities lead to greater disparities in educational attainment, job security, wealth distribution, and healthcare access among minority populations. Furthermore, bias-driven decision-making from employers also widens the wage gap between whites and minorities. In this way, it is easy to see how racial bias directly affects the economic stability of individuals and entire communities *(Leary & Robinson, 2018)*.

One example of racial bias can be found in the criminal justice system. Research has shown that people of color are disproportionately arrested, imprisoned, and sentenced more harshly when compared to their white counterparts *(Mitchell, 2020)*. This bias can often be attributed to systemic racism: the *"sets of institutional and individual behaviors, practices, and attitudes that operate within a society to benefit the dominant group and oppress members of other social groups"* (Leary &

Robinson, 2018). Such cases of racial bias often lead to disparities in the criminal justice system, in which people of color are over-policed and over-criminalized due to their background or ethnicity.

Gender

Gender biases are prejudiced or stereotyped beliefs about the roles, behaviors, and characteristics of men and women in society. These beliefs shape how individuals perceive and delineate the roles and attributes people of a particular gender should play. These biases are based on traditional and cultural values that assume the roles and characteristics of males and females are set in stone.

For example, one of the most commonly known gender biases is the notion that women are inherently inferior to men. This belief is rooted in traditional gender roles that assume men are naturally better at tasks that require physical strength and intellectual prowess. At the same time, women are seen as less capable when it comes to educational, political, and professional power. This bias has long been reflected in the wage gap between men and women, with women earning only 83 cents for every dollar men earn *(Iacurci, 2022)*.

Another gender bias is the gender stereotype that men should be breadwinners and women should be homemakers due to traditional gender roles. This stereotype contributes to the problem of the gender wage gap because it implies that certain jobs are only *"suitable"* for men, such as those jobs that pay more. Also, women's contributions as homemakers are devalued.

Economic

Economic biases refer to the tendencies of individuals or groups to act and make biased economic decisions due to cognitive, emotional, and institutional factors. Cognitive biases mean people can be influenced by their beliefs, leading them to make irrational economic decisions. In contrast, emotional biases often lead people to favor decisions that provide short-term satisfaction even if they are not economically sound in the long run. Institutional biases manifest in government, business, or other organizations that favor particular outcomes, even if those outcomes are not the most economically efficient or beneficial for all parties.

An example of an economic bias is the sunk cost fallacy, wherein people are unwilling to accept losses. Also, they continue to invest more resources because they believe investing more will enable them to recoup their losses or lead to a better outcome. This fallacy often leads to a cycle of sunk costs, where people use up more resources that have no chance of recovery, even though it might be more rational and economically beneficial to cut their losses and move on.

For instance, a business may continue to invest in a doomed project due to the sunk cost of the previous investments, even though those investments are unlikely to be recovered. This results in the company expending more resources which would be better spent investing in a more financially sound venture *(Chen, Lao, & McCue, 2019)*.

Another example of an economic bias is the endowment bias. It is a cognitive bias in which people tend to attribute more value to items they own than to identical items they do not own. This cognitive bias is often associated with an unwillingness to part with possessions. Likewise, this bias originates from personal identity and the fact that people experience loss more heavily than gain. Additionally, this bias can also be formed from the belief that objects have sentimental value.

For example, when deciding whether to sell a car that has been in a family for many years, the owner may be unwilling to part with it, although a similar vehicle can be found online for a much lower price. This is because the owner has an emotional attachment to the car and thus endows it with a higher value than it would otherwise hold. They may even be willing to pay more than necessary to keep it, reflecting their identity and the sentimental value they attach to it.

How to Avoid Making Assumptions and Biases

The ability to think critically is essential for making well-informed decisions. A critical thinker can analyze situations and evidence objectively and draw valid conclusions from the facts. However, when your mind wanders, assumptions and biases can cloud your perspective and lead to potentially erroneous assumptions and conclusions.

This section of our book will examine ways to avoid making assumptions and biases in critical thinking and learn to train your mind to be rational and analytical. We will discuss how to identify and overcome personal biases, evaluate information objectively, and identify when your opinion and assumptions affect your thoughts.

Become Fully Engaged

Staying fully engaged in critical thinking can help eliminate assumptions and biases by encouraging a more thorough examination of the issue or argument. When fully engaged in problem-solving discussions, we actively listen and consider all sides of the issue. Plus, we ponder potential solutions without making assumptions or drawing immediate conclusions. This facilitates an open dialogue that allows for exchanging ideas and perspectives. Also, it opens up opportunities for challenge and debate of existing and overlooked solutions. Such situations encourage us to think beyond the presented information. Likewise, to consider alternative solutions that may address the problem more effectively.

By staying engaged in the discussion, we can more easily recognize when assumptions and biases are used in the decision. As such, it lets us make a process, allowing for potential solutions to be identified and discussed without being dismissed due to a preconceived belief or notion. Staying fully engaged in critical thinking can also foster a better understanding of the issue or argument, which can minimize the influence of any assumptions or biases that may have been present. Similarly, staying engaged will help ensure that the problem-solving process is conducted with a more open mind. Likewise, it gives us a greater awareness of the impact of assumptions and biases on the issue or argument.

Practice Reflection

A reflection is an important tool in critical thinking because it helps us identify, process, and discuss our assumptions and biases. Reflective thinking allows us to critically analyze our beliefs, values, and assumptions by considering their validity, accuracy, and appropriateness. This helps to ensure we are not making assumptions or coming to conclusions based on incorrect information or unfounded beliefs.

When we frequently reflect on our assumptions, thoughts, and biases, we can become more aware of how our biases and preconceived notions may influence our decisions and behavior. As we reflect upon our thoughts and assumptions, we can begin to challenge them. Doing so will help us recognize and eliminate erroneous assumptions that may influence our view on a certain matter.

In addition, reflection can also help us to uncover hidden assumptions. By reflecting upon our opinions and beliefs, we can often identify implicit beliefs or assumptions influencing our behavior or thoughts. Recognizing these assumptions can help to increase our understanding of an issue or situation and enable us to adjust our thinking to understand better and appreciate different perspectives. With continual practice, reflection can help to sharpen critical thinking skills, allowing us to understand better, analyze, and respond to any issue or situation.

Actively Question Ideas

Everyone needs to view information objectively rather than merely relying on their personal beliefs. When actively questioning ideas, we take the time to reconsider assumptions and biases, analyze the evidence, and consider different perspectives. This process can help us uncover faults in our thinking and identify potential flaws in our arguments. By examining and challenging assumptions and biases, we can better understand the complexities of the situation and come to more informed and objective conclusions.

When actively questioning ideas, focus on the validity of the evidence rather than your own opinion. Also, consider alternate perspectives and examine the potential outcomes of different scenarios. This way, you can better determine the potential consequences of your decisions and assess the validity of your conclusions.

Actively questioning ideas also requires us to accept that our assumptions and biases may be wrong. Likewise, we should be willing to put aside our preconceived notions and open our minds to alternative suggestions. Aside from that, we should analyze the evidence with an unbiased outlook and evaluate the reliability of the sources. Taking the time to challenge assumptions and biases actively helps us to make well-informed decisions based on verifiable evidence rather than personal opinion.

Exercise Humility

Exercising humility and modesty is necessary for thinking critically. Practicing humility when engaging in critical thinking can help eliminate assumptions and biases. As such, humility allows us to step back and look at our conclusions and opinions objectively. Besides that, it lets us consider different perspectives and views. Humility also encourages us to challenge personal biases and assumptions that influence evaluating and assessing the evidence. Without being aware of our biases and assumptions, we may be unable to make rational judgments and draw conclusions that do not accurately reflect the facts.

Humility also encourages us to recognize the limits of our knowledge and expertise. Likewise, it helps distinguish between fact and opinion, acknowledges the impact of biases and assumptions, and considers the possibility that our conclusions may be wrong. In addition, it allows us to seek out and accept feedback from others, even if it differs from our interpretations. As such, it makes us remain open to feedback, wherein we are more likely to come to a well-rounded conclusion based on various opinions.

For example, consider the hypothetical story of a teacher named Jane and a particularly difficult student named John. Jane feels frustrated and, without giving John the benefit of the doubt, assumes that he is deliberately trying to act out and give her a hard time. Yet, by practicing humility, Jane can take a step back to gain a better understanding of the situation. She speaks to John privately and addresses her concerns calmly and respectfully. When John explains that he has been feeling overwhelmed by schoolwork, Jane can empathize with his situation. She understands that his misbehavior may not have been intentional but rather a result of his stress with the school. Despite her status as a teacher, Jane decided to humble herself, allowing her to understand John's situation better, leading to a better solution for both parties. Moreover, she was reminded of the importance of not making assumptions and being open to whatever the situation may bring.

Ultimately, exercising humility can help us make rational, unbiased decisions by allowing us to evaluate information with an open mind, remain objective and impartial, and recognize the potential flaws in our assumptions and biases. Humility can also improve our critical thinking skills and help us become better communicators. By allowing ourselves to consider the evidence and opinions of others objectively, we can come to a more well-informed and informed conclusion than we could have on our own.

Chapter 8:
Evaluating Data

Data evaluation is a critical part of the critical thinking process. It involves the assessment of the significance and relevance of collected evidence to the conclusion being drawn. Evaluating data for significance and relevance is a key step in producing more accurate assessments, as it helps prevent incorrect assumptions from being made. It involves examining the accuracy, reliability, and validity of the data itself, as well as considering the possible biases of the data collector and the relevance of the data to the issue being discussed. In addition, data evaluation can help to clarify the results, allowing decisions to be made that are well-informed and transparent. Evaluating the significance and relevance of data aids in identifying the most appropriate solution to any particular problem and allows us to discern whether an existing solution works or should be replaced with a different option.

In this chapter, we will talk about the methodologies behind data evaluation and how one can gauge the reliability of acquired data. We will also discuss how we can weigh competing information and evidence against one another. Aside from that, we will delve deeper into the relationships between evidence and any given claim or argument.

Reliability of the Data

The reliability of data is an essential part of critical thinking. Reliable data provides the necessary information to form evidence-based conclusions, make sound decisions, and draw valid inferences and is integral to the process of reasoning. Data reliability increases trust and credibility in the outcome, as well as technical accuracy and credibility. Without reliable data, the analyses of information and thought processes become more subject to personal bias and prejudices. Data reliability is a measure of the accuracy and consistency of data over time. It is important in critical thinking because it ensures the validity of evidence used in the decision-making process. Unreliable data can lead to incorrect conclusions, costing time and resources, and missing key strategic opportunities.

Data that is reliable is accurate, representative of the data population, and collected with consistent methods and tools. In addition to accuracy and conformity, it is essential to determine if the data is comprehensive to support the outcome or research. Examining the data sources to ensure they are unbiased and validated is also necessary. Finally, data reliability implies that the data should be free from errors and it should also be secure. Data that is corrupted, or not adequately secured from malicious actors, can yield unreliable outcomes, especially in sensitive data contexts like healthcare. Therefore, it is vital to ensure that the data collected, stored, and used is trustworthy and secure.

The 4 Pillars of Critical Thinking

Significance and Relevance of Information

Information is essential to critical thinking, as it furnishes us with the data to evaluate different perspectives and make educated decisions. A critical thinker gathers reliable data, assesses its credibility, evaluates bias and relevance, and then weighs the evidence to arrive at a well-rounded conclusion. Critical thinkers also reflect on their understanding of the information and its consequences, coming to logical conclusions.

The information to support critical thinking must be valid, relevant, and significant to produce reliable results. To assess the legitimacy of gathered information, it is essential to inspect its source. Information from reliable sources such as peer-reviewed literature, government and institutional documents, and industry experts is generally more convincing than information found in public forums, which can often be biased, incomplete, or untrue *(Bowell et al., 2020)*.

When engaging in critical thinking, evaluating the source of information and determining its relevance and significance is essential. This helps ensure that only relevant data is used in decision-making, eliminating unnecessary resources spent on irrelevant or insignificant information. Relevant data directly affect the issue at hand and could influence the conclusion. In contrast, irrelevant or insignificant information does not contribute to the outcome *(Bowell et al., 2020)*. Considering these critical thinking components, decisions can be made more efficiently and effectively.

Relationship Between Evidence and Claim

Arguments are statements made to prove or disprove a point. They are claims backed up with reasons and evidence, which are facts that support the argument. Examples of reasons and evidence may include statistics, surveys, studies, experiments, anecdotes, and quotes. Typically, arguments are introduced with a statement showing the opinion or belief followed by reasons and evidence showing why the information is true or false. In this section of the book, we will further explore the relationships between claims and evidence and how they contribute to sound arguments.

Again, a claim refers to an assertion, typically expressing an opinion or belief. This is often presented in the context of an argument. Claims are usually substantiated with evidence to support a particular position or perspective. For a claim to be considered valid, it must be backed by factual data and logical reasoning.

For example, if a person is trying to claim that *"climate change is real,"* they must offer evidence to support their assertion. This could include scientific evidence such as reports from the United Nations Intergovernmental Panel on Climate Change, climate scientists' data, or reputable sources like NASA. Supporting evidence could also include facts about changes in the global temperature, sea levels, and other measurements suggesting that the Earth's climate was not in the same state before the industrial revolution. Yet, this claim is only considered valid if it is supported by solid evidence and credible sources.

Meanwhile, a reason is a statement that explains or justifies a claim. Reasons supply evidence and logic that present why the claim is valid. For instance, a student may argue that schools should make recess mandatory for all students. To support this claim, the student might offer several reasons, such as *"recess provides an opportunity for physical activity, helps relieve stress and anxiety, and encourages creative thinking and problem-solving abilities."* By providing evidence for the claim and demonstrating why it is true, the student has effectively used reasons to support their argument.

Shreds of evidence related to your argument help support the reasons and claims. Hence, evidence is crucial to critical thinking, providing factual support for assertions, opinions, and conclusions. Evidence, in this context, can take various forms, such as facts, statistics, quotes from experts, testimonies of witnesses, and more. By providing solid evidence to back up the reasons and claims being made in a critical thinking exercise, the validity and robustness of the argument are significantly increased.

An example of how evidence relates to argumentation can be seen in a debate concerning the effectiveness of a particular drug for treating a certain illness. In such a scenario, one side may claim that the drug is effective in treating the illness, supported by evidence in the form of scientific studies, peer-reviewed journal articles, testimonies from medical professionals, records from pharmaceutical companies, and more. Likewise, the other side could present evidence that the drug is ineffective, such as testimonies from patients who have tried the drug and did not receive any benefit, studies showing the ineffectiveness of the medicine in treating the illness, or similar supporting evidence. In any case, both sides make claims with an evidence-based foundation, thus making the critical thinking exercise all the more meaningful.

Weighing Competing Evidence and Information

Critical thinking requires an individual to have an open mind and to be willing to evaluate multiple pieces of evidence to make an informed decision. When engaging in critical thinking, it is vital not to take any one piece of evidence as the absolute truth. Instead, weighing the competing evidence against one another is essential to find the best solution. Likewise, be objective, logical, and impartially assess the evidence to form a conclusion.

When weighing the evidence, consider each piece on its merit and concerning other evidence. It is essential to consider all relevant details, facts, and perspectives to create an informed opinion. This will help ensure that the evidence is balanced and that a conclusion is not reached without appropriate scrutiny. At the same time, it is also essential to be aware of any bias when considering the evidence. Bias can be present in collecting and assessing information, so it is vital to be mindful of potential bias and take steps to mitigate it.

Before discussing the methodologies in weighing competing evidence, we must examine what constitutes reliable evidence and the different types of evidence available to us: *corroborating, convergent, contradictory, and conflicting.*

Corroborating evidence supports a conclusion or argument made by another piece of evidence or testimony. Also, this evidence is typically gathered by interviewing witnesses, reviewing documents, and analyzing physical evidence. In many instances, corroborating evidence gives additional power to a person's claims or arguments by demonstrating that another source has reached the same conclusion.

Meanwhile, convergent evidence is evidence gathered from multiple sources or methods and provides numerous confirmations of the same conclusion. This type of evidence is usually used to support a hypothesis or theory, to suggest that the data collected from one source is reliable and accurate.

Then, contradictory evidence is evidence that shows data or information from one source contradicts data or information from another source. This evidence highlights potential inconsistencies in the data or arguments and can signal the need for further investigation.

Lastly, conflicting evidence directly contradicts a previously accepted argument or position. This type of evidence is not necessarily wrong but may point to issues with the current understanding of a particular issue or topic. Besides that, conflicting evidence can support a change in the current understanding or confirm that the original position is correct.

However, not all evidence is worthy of one's attention. As such, any significant or relevant evidence should have relevance, believability, and probative force. That said, relevance is a fundamental property of evidence that determines if the evidence is pertinent to the case or issue. It is up to the thinker or analyst to decide the relevance of evidence, and they will decide this by considering both the nature of the evidence and the purpose it is being presented for.

Believability is the second fundamental property of evidence. This is the trustworthiness of the evidence and whether its accuracy or truth can be depended upon. The believability of any given piece of evidence will depend upon the circumstances. For example, witness testimony may be more believable if it is consistent with other evidence or given from an expert or reliable source.

Furthermore, probative force is the third and final fundamental property of evidence. This is the ability of a piece of evidence to prove a particular point or issue. For evidence to be considered to have any probative force, it must be logically connected to the problem it is trying to prove. For instance, if an expert witness in a court case testifies that an object is the cause of an incident, there must be a logical connection between the object and the incident for it to have probative force.

Sir Francis Bacon's Methodology

Sir Francis Bacon's methodology of weighing evidence is a practical approach to developing judgments. This methodology utilizes Bacon's inductive reasoning, which involves using a series of observations to draw generalizations or conclusions. His practice includes several steps: *gathering evidence, analyzing the available evidence, and evaluating the evidence before coming to conclusions.* Working through this method step-by-step aids in developing an objective perspective when making decisions.

The first step in Bacon's methodology is to gather evidence. Analyzing all available evidence, including existing precedents and past experiences, is essential during this step. As such, it involves looking for causes of events, examining correlations, and assessing the strengths and weaknesses of various courses of action. This step aims to amass as much relevant evidence as possible to make an educated decision.

Once collected, the evidence must be analyzed to determine its reliability, accuracy, and relevance. For instance, be critical of the data, noting any inconsistencies or flaws, citing any sources that might be biased, and recognizing any factors that might influence the data. Doing so is essential to come to more reliable conclusions.

Finally, the evidence must be evaluated and compared to determine its usefulness. Subsequently, it requires considering the data's strengths and weaknesses, checking data points against each other, and determining if any correlations may exist between evidence points. With this step, you can develop a comprehensive view of the available data, allowing for a better-informed decision.

The Bayes' Theorem

Bayes' theorem is a type of probability theory that is used in forecasting or predicting. It is based on the foundation that the most reasonable outcome is the one with the largest probability. Likewise, it weighs competing evidence and can be used to calculate the probability of an event based on the evidence presented. Often, it is used in the legal field when determining the likelihood of a defendant being guilty or innocent.

The Bayes Theorem is expressed as: $P(A|B) = (P(B|A) \times P(A))/P(B)$

Let us look at an example to understand how Bayes' theorem works. For instance, Jane believes that she has a medical condition. As such, she can use Bayes' theorem to evaluate the strength of her belief. Imagine Jane visited her doctor and was given a test to determine if she was suffering from the condition in question. If the test gives a positive result, then Jane can use Bayes' theorem to calculate the probability of her belief being correct.

Where P(A) is the probability that Jane has the condition before the test, and P(B|A) is the probability of a positive test result given where P(A) is true. P(B) is the probability of a positive test result regardless of P(A).

By considering all these factors, Jane can use Bayes' theorem to determine the probability that her belief is correct. However, this theorem still has several detractors who criticize its methodology. The first criticism of Bayes' theorem is its limited scope. For instance, this theorem can calculate the probability of only one event occurring. Even if additional information is included, the theorem does not indicate the new information's reliability. Therefore, it is challenging to make predictions about more than one event.

Another issue with Bayes' theorem is that it relies on prior knowledge or beliefs. While this can be a helpful guide for making accurate predictions, it can also be subject to biases and errors. Therefore, the results of the theorem can be inaccurate and misleading if the prior knowledge or beliefs used are unreliable. In addition, the theorem is based on a single assumption, namely that all variables are independent. Hence, although it may be true in some cases, it cannot be assumed true in all cases, so information can be missed or distorted when using the theorem.

Dempster and Shafer's Theory of Evidence

The Dempster-Shafer Theory of Evidence (DST) is a mathematical framework for determining a statement or hypothesis's degree of belief. It was developed by Arthur P. Dempster and Glenn Shafer in 1976 and is based on subjective probability. DST is based on the idea that a person's beliefs and evidence can be used to reason and make decisions. It combines evidence from multiple sources to form an overall conclusion.

Using a numerical scale, the theory assigns a number to each piece of evidence, called the *"degree of belief"* or *"belief mass."* This number indicates how confident one is that the evidence is valid. For example, if one has a belief mass of 0.7 for the statement *"the sky is blue,"* then one believes the statement is true to a high degree of probability. This belief mass can be updated using other evidence, such as witness statements or test results. The updated belief mass can then be combined with the existing belief mass to form an overall conclusion about the statement. The overall conclusion is then expressed as a probability, ranging from 0 to 1, to indicate the degree of belief in the statement.

Likewise, the Dempster-Shafer evidence theory has its fair share of criticisms. Firstly, it has been criticized for its complexity. The Dempster-Shafer theory requires complex calculations and assumptions, which limit the ability of the average user to implement it. Additionally, there is the potential for borderline cases and ambiguity when computing the belief and plausibility functions because of multiple possible solutions. Aside from that, the Dempster-Shafer theory does not consider the dynamics of interactions between system components. This can lead to incorrect results in situations where more information is available than the system uses. It also implies that new evidence can only be incorporated into the system slowly. Lastly, the Dempster-Shafer theory is limited by its inability to handle conflicting evidence. As such, it cannot easily handle situations where different pieces of evidence provide opposing conclusions. Similarly, this methodology cannot take inherently incomplete or contradictory evidence.

Despite these criticisms, the Dempster-Shafer theory is still widely used and accepted. As long as its limitations are considered, it can still be an effective tool in making decisions where data is sparse or uncertain.

Chapter 9:
Draw Conclusions or Solutions

To conclude our discussion on the process pillar of critical thinking, we will discuss what it means to draw logical conclusions and solutions. By referring to several theoretical frameworks and studies, this chapter aims to provide insight into the effective tools and strategies needed to recognize, analyze, and reflect on the consequences of individual decisions. It will also offer practical advice on how to evaluate the consequences of a decision before pursuing a particular solution. Through the use of different approaches, such as brainstorming, goal setting, and problem-solving, this chapter will explore the processes of drawing meaningful conclusions and solutions to understand the implications of a problem.

Additionally, the chapter will also briefly discuss the importance of self-assessment and collaboration in the decision-making process, which can serve as a perfect segue into the next pillar of critical thinking. By emphasizing the need to collaborate with others and consider their perspectives, this chapter will illustrate how working together can provide a more comprehensive understanding of a situation and lead to better outcomes. As such, by focusing on the in-depth analysis and critical evaluation of evidence, you will learn how to efficiently and effectively reach a conclusion or solution.

The Purpose of Drawing Conclusions

The purpose of generating solutions and conclusions in the critical thinking process is to determine a course of action to address a particular problem and evaluate the potential outcomes of taking a certain action. It involves assessing evidence, identifying the most critical issues, and analyzing possible courses of action.

When generating solutions, critical thinkers consider the strengths and weaknesses of all the options, the situation at hand, and any potential implications of those options. All information must be analyzed carefully, and all possible solutions must be weighed before any definitive action is taken.

Generating conclusions involves synthesizing and reexamining the information in light of new evidence. This process helps determine the most likely outcome regarding short-term and long-term impacts. As critical thinkers, we must ensure that their conclusions are logical and consistent with their initial objectives.

Remember that critical thinking is a process of actively analyzing, synthesizing, and evaluating information to draw logical conclusions. When we cannot draw any solutions or conclusions, the process of critical thinking is rendered moot because the core objective has not been met. In this case, we cannot assess the various components of the problem. Therefore, we cannot work toward any meaningful resolution. Without the ability to analyze information, draw valid conclusions, generate alternative solutions and evaluate their efficacy, critical thinking is ineffective and cannot contribute to solving the issue.

The 4 Pillars of Critical Thinking

Factors that Influence Solution Generation

Many factors can influence the outcome of drawing solutions and conclusions. For instance, a person's level of knowledge and experience may significantly impact their ability to generate effective solutions to a given problem. If a person has little knowledge or experience on the subject, they may be unable to recognize the details necessary to make an informed decision. However, a person with more knowledge and experience may better evaluate the information, weigh the pros and cons of different solutions, and make wise decisions.

An individual's mindset is also an essential factor in solution generation. Optimistic and confident people may be better able to see potential solutions, think outside the box, and develop creative solutions. It involves analyzing the problem from different angles and perspectives, generating new ideas, and combining other elements to create a viable solution. This can be done by brainstorming ideas and researching alternative solutions to find an answer that no one has yet discovered. Likewise, it requires an open mind, flexibility, and a willingness to experiment and push the boundaries to find the best solution. On the other hand, someone who has a pessimistic outlook may be more likely to focus on obstacles and believe that no solution is possible.

Moreover, our perspectives can also influence the outcome. Different perspectives can help to identify potential solutions and weaknesses in existing ones. For example, the perspective of someone who has a diverse cultural background may be able to offer alternative approaches which another person may not have considered. Finally, motivation is an influential factor. A person who is motivated to find a solution and willing to put in the effort to get there is likelier to succeed than someone disinterested and unwilling to do the work.

The Stages of Drawing Solutions

Solving problems or making decisions often involves stages that can guide us toward reaching effective and optimal solutions. By following this framework, we can improve our problem-solving skills, make more informed decisions, and achieve better outcomes in various areas of life.

Identifying the Problem

Identifying the problem is the first step in drawing a conclusion or solution. This involves determining the issue and why it needs to be addressed. When identifying the problem, be analytical and break it down into its components to ensure that the essential elements of the problem are identified.

For example, imagine you are tasked with developing a solution to reduce litter in a park. The first step would be to identify the problem. To do this, you must assess the situation and understand what is causing the littering. This could involve looking at recent data on littering in the park, talking to park visitors, assessing the available garbage bins, etc. After completing the investigation, it may become clear that the issue is that visitors are unaware of the bins in the park, leading them to discard their trash on the ground.

In such situations, looking at the problem from all angles and gaining detailed knowledge of the issue is essential. This can be done by asking questions, researching related topics, and talking to those involved. Doing this lets you understand the problem and how it should be approached.

Defining Objectives

Once the problem has been identified, it is time to determine the solution's desired outcome. This stage involves setting goals and objectives that must be met for the plan to move forward. To define these objectives, ask yourself what you intend to achieve by finding a conclusion or solution.

For example, suppose a company is focused on increasing efficiency. In that case, objectives include decreasing expenses and waste, optimizing workflow and processes, and utilizing data-driven decisions whenever possible. Additionally, creating a comprehensive and detailed list of measurable metrics will help ensure maximum efficiency with minimal resources. The more specific each metric is determined beforehand, the smoother the process of achieving those goals becomes.

Aside from that, time management is crucial in efficient problem-solving, especially when working with complex problems or large teams. Allocating sufficient time at the project's start and throughout its course will allow any hurdles encountered along the way to be addressed. Likewise, it lets additional tasks or strategies be implemented as needed.

Meanwhile, in the context of problem-solving within a government entity, officials should create concrete, specific, and achievable objectives that measure the successful completion of the solution and are aligned with the problem being solved. The objectives should outline success criteria, include completion timelines, and establish the goal to minimize any issues related to the problem. For example, the government may face the problem of high unemployment in a particular region. To address this problem, government officials would first identify the causes of the high unemployment rate, as discussed in the previous step. As such, it could include a lack of job opportunities, a mismatch between the skills of the workers and the jobs available, or inadequate support services.

From there, the government can then define the objectives of its problem-solving efforts. In this case, an objective would be to increase opportunities for employment among the population. Another objective would be to facilitate skills-building among employable individuals. These are just some simple examples of objectives that could provide further insight and direction to probable solutions.

Investigating Possible Solutions

Crafting an effective solution to a problem often starts with brainstorming, which works best when the group is diverse. This can be challenging in the workplace, mainly when employees are from different departments and have different perspectives or experiences. But, introducing diversity-oriented initiatives such as promoting more diverse opinions, including underrepresented voices in decision-making processes, and facilitating cross-departmental dialogue through regular check-ins can help foster a collaborative environment and increase workplace productivity.

Moreover, knowing the potential impacts of any potential solution is paramount to understanding how best to address a communication issue. As such, tailored research should be conducted to provide more insight. This could involve analysis of existing literature, interviews with stakeholders or expert advisors, and collaboration among team members. In this way, a comprehensive picture can be built regarding possible solutions and their likely associated outcomes.

Likewise, effective communication is essential for the successful functioning of any organization. To ensure the most appropriate action, information must be gathered from internal and external sources. This may include examining scholarly papers about organizational development techniques, speaking to an industry leader for their perspective, or encouraging open dialogue between team members. Such measures will help form a better understanding of the problem itself so that a more informed decision may be made.

The next step towards finding the right solution is analyzing the available options. Every potential solution should be thoroughly researched before being adopted. This process involves looking at the pros and cons of each option to determine which option has the highest potential for success while minimizing risk. Additionally, it helps to identify any hidden or unforeseen issues that may arise in the future.

Finally, once a viable solution has been identified, keep track of its progress and adjust if needed. Regular performance evaluations provide key insights into how well a solution works and whether any additional improvements could be made. Ultimately, this will ensure that a suitable outcome is achieved within an acceptable timeframe while avoiding any costly mistakes that could occur due to a lack of oversight or preparation.

Evaluating Solutions

Once possible solutions have been identified and gathered, they should be evaluated to determine the best path forward. All solutions should be analyzed and assessed based on efficiency, costs, time, and impact in this stage. As such, evaluating solutions involves assessing the pros and cons of each proposed solution and determining how effectively it addresses the original problem.

To do this, the decision-maker must examine each possible solution and weigh its benefits and drawbacks. Once all solutions have been evaluated, the decision-maker should select the best option that meets all requirements with the least drawbacks.

For instance, imagine a company is trying to decide how to increase its profits. The company has considered three possible solutions, each with its advantages and disadvantages:

Solution 1: Cut back on salaries and reduce staff.

Advantages: Increased profits due to cost savings of wages and staff reduction.

Disadvantages: Potential loss of motivated employees, decreased morale, and difficulty finding new talent.

Solution 2: Increase the price of products and services.

Advantages: Increased revenue due to higher prices and potential reduction in costs associated with staffing and salaries.

Disadvantages: Possible decrease in demand due to increased prices and potential reduction in market share.

Solution 3: Develop new products and services.

Advantages: Could increase revenue and sales due to new products and services.

Disadvantages: Takes time to research, develop, and implement new products, potentially leading to delays in implementation and increased costs.

In this example, the decision-maker must evaluate each potential solution and weigh the pros and cons to determine which is best for the company. This could involve looking at the financial implications of each solution, the potential risks, and any other factors that could affect the implementation of the solution. After comparing the solutions, the decision-maker can choose the one with the least drawbacks and the greatest potential benefits.

Finalizing Solutions

The final step in the process is to determine a suitable solution and put it into action. This involves acquiring all the necessary materials and creating an implementation plan. Once chosen, ensure you have access to the resources, tools, and approaches needed to bring your solution to fruition.

Furthermore, this stage of the process is pivotal in achieving success as it requires thoughtfulness and consideration for potential roadblocks along the way. As such, be aware of any potential risks associated with making a specific decision before proceeding, as this could lead to costly setbacks further down the line.

Proactively anticipating situations before making decisions can ensure your solutions succeed and meet expected outcomes. With careful consideration at every step, you can ensure that your decisions result in meaningful change and real progress.

Pillar 3:
Improvement

Improvement is essential to critical thinking, aiding individuals in developing their analytical and cognitive abilities. By evaluating and refining ideas or solutions, individuals can challenge themselves to think differently and consider alternative perspectives. This requires careful analysis of existing solutions and modifications based on new information or insights. Through improvement, individuals can identify potential weaknesses while exploring new solutions and ways of approaching a problem.

Problem-solving techniques, such as brainstorming and problem-solving analysis, can be employed to help individuals reach their goals. Furthermore, improvement is not restricted to only the creative or analytical stages. As such, it can span both areas and thus enhance the individual's understanding of the entire process.

The benefits of improvement reach beyond simply improving one's thinking ability. A well-thought-out plan of action increases the chances of achieving desired outcomes by allowing the individual to use reliable data gathered during the evaluation stage to formulate better decisions. Additionally, personalized approaches adapted from diverse sources can give users more flexibility in finding the best solutions.

Moreover, improving critical thinking involves much more than just gaining knowledge. In addition to informing yourself and actively seeking new solutions, it also requires deliberate self-reflection. This involves examining one's thought process to identify any pre-existing biases or false assumptions that could lead to unsuccessful decision-making.

By understanding and identifying these mental blocks, individuals can develop more reliable ways of interpreting and analyzing data. One way of doing this is using heuristics, mental shortcuts that help us prioritize ideas quickly. These take the form of rules of thumb that can be used to make quicker decisions without necessarily having all the information at hand.

In addition, deliberate practice can improve critical thinking, such as simulations and roleplays, which use real-world scenarios to refine our solutions and analyze our decisions. Doing so allows us to simulate different situations, test our responses beforehand, and react accordingly when encountering similar situations. Ultimately, improvement demands a combination of active knowledge-seeking and reflective practice, enabling people to think critically and make better decisions in their daily lives.

Chapter 10:
Self-Reflection in Critical Thinking

Self-reflection is crucial for performing effective critical thinking. We can use it to reflect on our current knowledge and question our assumptions, allowing us to make better decisions. Developing this skill requires introspection, where we focus on our thoughts, feelings, and beliefs. This can help uncover unconscious biases, assess evidence validity, and explore alternative perspectives.

The process of self-reflection also encourages us to consider all parts of a situation before concluding. This includes looking at the effects of our actions, the implications of our ideas, and possible alternative paths that could be taken. By re-evaluating our thoughts, we can gain insight into how we form opinions and identify weaknesses in our reasoning process.

Finally, engaging in self-reflection allows us to assess the quality and accuracy of our solutions for any given problem or task. Doing so can help us understand how we create meaning from different pieces of information and adjust or revise aspects of our thinking as required. Incorporating this method into everyday activities can increase accuracy when making decisions.

Altogether, self-reflection aims to bring conscious awareness to our thinking process, allowing us to challenge our internal biases and beliefs. Taking the time to self-reflect enables us to identify weaknesses in our thinking and craft more meaningful and accurate solutions.

Why Self-Reflection Is Important

Self-reflection is an essential practice for leading a more meaningful and fulfilling life. It allows us to become aware of our biases, challenge our assumptions, and make changes for the better. Aside from that, self-reflection can improve decision-making, increase empathy, and boost creativity.

Taking time to reflect on our beliefs and behaviors can also help us become conscious of our influence within society. For instance, evaluating how our actions affect air quality or marine life allows us to make conscious choices based on their potential impact. Additionally, considering this information often results in smarter and more mindful decisions. Likewise, it helps us develop a much fuller understanding of how our actions shape the world around us.

Besides that, self-reflection can also lead to significant advancements in personal development by allowing us to understand our deep thoughts, feelings, and behavior patterns. This process helps us recognize when irrational or unconscious thought patterns may influence our actions and allows us to make more conscious choices that better serve long-term goals.

Moreover, regular self-reflection encourages greater self-awareness, which helps facilitate acceptance of individual qualities, both weaknesses and strengths, without fear or judgment. With this knowledge, we are better positioned to pursue growth opportunities that align with our core values and ultimately lead us toward lives filled with meaning and satisfaction.

Subsequently, self-reflection is a powerful tool for personal growth, allowing us to recognize our strengths and weaknesses. By taking the time to look within ourselves, we can identify areas of improvement and develop strategies that allow us to reach our goals. Likewise, it is also an invaluable way to understand our behavior in different situations, as it helps us recognize both our motivations and triggers.

When we practice self-reflection, it can help create breakthroughs in thinking and awareness. Through this process of self-examination, we gain insight into why we act in certain ways or react in particular situations. Understanding can empower us to make conscious changes to improve our mental health and well-being.

In addition to aiding personal growth, self-reflection is an effective means for learning from mistakes. By analyzing our thoughts and behaviors, we can pinpoint where things have gone wrong and devise more effective problem-solving techniques. With such knowledge, we are better equipped to change the course of negative patterns to reach desired outcomes better.

Not only does it allow us to build more efficient problem-solving skills. Yet, the reflective practice provides a platform for looking at past occurrences, allowing for further development. Such exercises enable synthesizing existing ideas and help individuals develop innovative solutions from different perspectives.

Breaking into the limits also involves gaining insight into our fear and anxiety. Self-reflection can help us identify our fears and understand how they may prevent us from achieving our goals. It allows us to recognize our anxieties and create strategies to manage them. This insight can be invaluable when working to break through our limits. Ultimately, self-reflection provides an opportunity for personal growth.

By reflecting on our experiences and evaluating our strengths and weaknesses, we can gain insight and understanding, which can be leveraged to become better versions of ourselves. Self-reflection can help us become more confident and self-aware and to break through the barriers that prevent us from reaching our goals and living our best lives.

Areas of Focus in Self-Reflection

Through self-reflection, we can identify our strengths and weaknesses. Likewise, it allows us to reflect on our thoughts and emotions and gain insight into our behaviors and actions. There are many areas of focus in self-reflection, including:

Logic and Reasoning

Logic and reasoning are often essential in problem-solving and decision-making. As such, it requires breaking down complex problems into small, manageable parts. Self-reflection can strengthen these skills by helping us look at our decisions objectively and identify patterns in our decision-making process. Through such practices, we can identify potential flaws in our reasoning, take steps to improve our thought processes, and make more sound decisions in the future.

To maximize the effectiveness of self-reflection for developing logic and reasoning skills, be mindful of individual biases. Certain cognitive biases may lead us to choose based on incorrect assumptions or flawed information. Awareness of these biases can help us recognize them when they arise and strive for objectivity while reflecting on past decisions.

Finally, proactive practice is needed to develop strong logic and reasoning skills. This includes activities such as reading books or articles related to critical thinking and mathematical exercises that involve forming deductive arguments from data or insights gained from observation. Additionally, playing games like chess or puzzles can help hone logical thought processes by making us think critically about our moves and strategies. Ultimately, regular practice allows us to become better equipped with the tools necessary for making thoughtful decisions now and in the future.

Self-Awareness

Self-awareness is a state of mind where individuals are conscious of their emotions, thoughts, and behaviors, and understand how these elements can influence others. This skill is essential for introspection, allowing one to gain insights into their actions, thoughts, and emotions. For instance, an employee feeling stressed due to numerous deadlines might take a moment to self-reflect and understand the cause of their stress. Through self-awareness, they might realize they are stressed because they have taken on more tasks than they can handle.

Engaging in self-reflection will allow us to investigate how their thoughts, emotions, and behaviors influence one another and how they interact with the environment. When developing self-awareness, self-reflection is essential for understanding how we respond to our circumstances and adapting our actions accordingly. From this, we can gain insight into our motivations, why we make certain decisions, and how to improve our behavior for greater effectiveness.

Awareness of Biases

Understanding biases and their impact on our decisions, thoughts, and beliefs is a crucial skill that should be developed to make well-informed choices. One's bias can be attributed to past experiences, culture, beliefs, and upbringing. Before forming an opinion or making any decision, it is essential to self-reflect and identify these potential biases that might influence our perception of the world. Questioning oneself about motives and reasons for the decisions can provide greater insight into one's beliefs and views, which can help foster understanding of different perspectives.

Biases play an influential role in communication and behavior, shaping how we interact with others. Acknowledging our biases can also lead to more open-minded discussions, allowing us to assess situations without being influenced by prejudices. Furthermore, recognizing the influence of various biases within social groups can help promote inclusivity in conversations, creating a more harmonious atmosphere by fostering mutual respect toward each other's opinions.

Changing deep-rooted prejudices is not easy. However, taking small steps toward developing awareness of our biases can create significant progress. Seeing people from all backgrounds as valuable members of society and taking responsibility for our actions are just some of these small steps that can lead to greater acceptance of diversity in today's world.

Tools for Self-Reflection

Developing self-reflection can help us make decisions based on our values and feelings. It involves taking an honest look at oneself and asking questions such as *"what am I learning from this?"* and *"what could I do better?"* Numerous tools are available that can assist us in developing those necessary skills, including.

Journaling

Writing a journal can be an effective means of self-expression, reflection, and introspection. Also, writing down our thoughts allows for improved mental clarity, problem-solving ability, and relief from negative emotions. In fact, journaling has been around for centuries, assisting people in exploring their inner thoughts and experiences through personal written narratives.

Aside from that, writing in a journal is not confined to any specific format. Instead, it encourages us to explore their feelings, thoughts, and experiences in our creative way. Similarly, it provides an opportunity to jot down the daily events, ponderings, or concerns about the current day and reflect on successes and challenges encountered during the day. Additionally, it gives the writer an avenue to plan future endeavors with detailed insight.

Aesthetic journaling is another popular form of journaling that incorporates art. This type of practice allows for creativity and exploration through visual illustration. People who engage in artful processes with words have found it helpful for sparking ideas and becoming more creative. Furthermore, incorporating art into our journal can provide an outlet for releasing difficult emotions. Ultimately, whatever method works best for an individual, writing regularly in any form, is an excellent means of self-reflection and understanding oneself better.

Ergo, journaling is a great way to foster personal growth and enhance self-awareness. Writing provides an opportunity to become acquainted with one's thoughts, feelings, and behaviors, which can lead to a greater understanding of oneself. It can also help recognize patterns in thinking and habits. Additionally, writing can be a powerful tool for managing challenging emotions and seeking constructive solutions.

Moreover, journaling can be employed as an artistic outlet, enabling us to articulate our ideas, dreams, tales, and perceptions distinctively and facilitate the development of a stronger self-identity. Furthermore, it is possible to use journaling for mission setting, breaking down significant objectives into achievable steps and tracking progress along the way. Regular journaling practice has been linked to improved decision-making abilities, reduced stress levels, and increased productivity. Thus, putting words on paper lets us gain perspective and make informed decisions.

Review of Past Experiences

Reviewing past experiences as a self-reflection tool is a process of taking the time to reflect on experiences that have been had and thinking about how it has impacted your life. This process allows you to look back on the experiences and their effects that have taken place in your life and how you have grown from them. It is a method of looking at how you have changed, grown, and developed since the experience occurred. To use this tool for self-reflection, you must begin by re-examining the experience and looking at what you learned from the situation. This can include looking at your feelings and thoughts during the experience, how they changed afterward, what mistakes were made, and what positive lessons were learned. Self-reflection can also include considering how the experience has changed how you view yourself and the world.

Next, you need to think about how you can use the experience to inform your future decisions. This exercise should also look at how the experience has impacted your mental and emotional health and how it has changed how you interact with people and situations. This could include looking at the big-picture impact the experience has had on your life and how it has shaped how you think and behave.

Taking the time to review past experiences can be an invaluable tool for self-reflection and personal growth. Not only can it help you to understand better and appreciate the changes you have gone through. Yet, it can also provide valuable insight into how you make decisions and the effects your decisions have on others. Likewise, it can be a powerful tool when reflecting on who you are and how you have changed and grown throughout life.

Mind Mapping

Mind mapping is a self-reflection tool that enables us to understand and analyze our thoughts, feelings, and experiences from a larger, more objective perspective. It allows us to map out our thoughts and feelings, linking them together in an organized fashion that reveals patterns, relationships, and trends. Aside from that, it also helps us gain insights into their internal world while, at the same time, providing a visual representation of the information. It limits personal biases and allows us to clarify personal identity and goals.

Moreover, mind mapping involves creating a visual diagram similar to a tree, with a central idea at the center and branches leading off the main concept. Each branch represents a different thought, feeling, idea, or experience, which can be further broken down into more specific details. This provides a comprehensive overview of the individual's internal world and a chance to explore different facets of the self. In addition to gaining insights, mind mapping helps individuals identify areas for self-improvement and personal growth. By visually displaying the information, individuals can easily identify areas that need work or further exploration. It is also helpful in setting goals and making plans for the future.

Chapter 11:
Role of Diverse Perspectives

Diverse perspectives play a crucial role in critical thinking by providing a variety of viewpoints and insights into a problem or situation. Having access to different perspectives helps us assess an issue from various angles and uncover deeper insights that we may not have considered otherwise.

Let us say a group is tasked with solving a particular problem. A diverse range of perspectives can allow the group to consider various options. For instance, a team member who is an expert in the specific field the issue relates to can give valuable insight into the problem. At the same time, a non-expert can provide a fresh perspective that might lead to an innovative solution. As such, a group member who frequently uses the system can offer their experience-based perspective, while a newcomer can highlight any system weaknesses they spot. Critically considering each of these diverse perspectives can help the group to discover the best solution to the problem.

Critical thinking is a highly valuable process of collecting and analyzing different information to draw meaningful conclusions. Broadening the range of perspectives contributes significantly to this process. Having a broader range of perspectives means looking at an issue or problem from different angles. It includes considering various perspectives, points of view, and experiences. Doing this helps expand knowledge by allowing for exploring the issue or problem from different sources and angles. This, in turn, can lead to more informed judgments and greater critical insight.

Additionally, broadening the range of perspectives encourages the consideration of multiple, sometimes contrary, opinions. It can provide a platform for a more open, constructive dialogue, enabling more meaningful interactions and more informed decision-making. Besides that, it gives interested parties a deeper understanding of the issue, allowing them to work towards mutually agreeable outcomes.

Overall, a more diverse and inclusive range of perspectives helps nurture the development of critical thinking. Drawing on different ideas, opinions, and experiences allows us to view the world through different lenses and push our critical thinking further. It encourages us to see the bigger picture and understand the issue more deeply. Ultimately, exposing ourselves to a broader range of perspectives helps us achieve more informed conclusions and makes us better, more effective critical thinkers.

Barriers to Diverse Perspectives in Critical Thinking

Preconceived notions and biases are mental filters that can impair one's ability to benefit from the perspectives of others. These prejudices can affect how one processes and evaluate data and information, harming critical thinking. They generally involve a fixed attitude or interpretive frame towards a person, event, or object.

The 4 Pillars of Critical Thinking

For example, suppose a person is biased toward members of a certain racial or ethnic group. In that case, they may unconsciously filter out information or ideas from that demographic. This may lead them to disregard valuable insights simply because the source does not fit within their existing framework.

In addition, pre-existing notions can lead to confirmation bias, where one only seeks out evidence and information supporting their existing beliefs while ignoring alternative viewpoints or evidence that does not fit their preconceptions. This tunnel vision can prevent one from critically evaluating all potential angles or perspectives, as it can limit the possibility of an unbiased approach to the issue or decision-making process at hand.

Moreover, preconceived notions and biases can be detrimental to critical thinking, as they can limit the potential for one to benefit from diverse perspectives or draw upon alternative ideas that could provide new insights or different solutions. It is important to detect and challenge biases and other mental filters, as this can broaden one's perspective and lead to a deeper understanding of the problem.

When there is a lack of recognition and acceptance of other perspectives, it can stymy one's ability to benefit from diverse perspectives and points of view. When someone does not recognize or accept the idea that a different perspective is valid, the value it can bring to the decision-making process is not considered when making a decision. This can lead to someone coming to a conclusion without considering multiple modes of thought or different points of view.

Without recognizing and accepting other perspectives, a person may ignore or dismiss different perspectives that could lead to better decisions in the long run. When this happens, it can limit the benefits of critical thinking as people will only look to what they think is right without considering different ideas, possibilities, or solutions. Without an open mind to accept others' views, any knowledge or insight they can offer will be disregarded, and the outcome of a decision will not reflect what could have been if all different perspectives were considered.

Overall, a lack of recognition and acceptance of other perspectives is a blockade to truly benefitting from diverse perspectives in critical thinking. Thus, people need to be open-minded and recognize the value that different perspectives can bring to decision-making.

Incorporating Diverse Perspectives into Critical Thinking

Critical listening is essential for engaging in critical thinking and accommodating diverse perspectives. It involves actively listening to others, considering and evaluating their ideas, avoiding bias and judgments, and asking open-ended questions. Developing critical listening skills requires practice and education to become proficient in understanding the points being made by others.

One example of why it is important to invest in critical listening skills is to ensure that different perspectives are heard and considered. For instance, in a classroom debate on the pros and cons of a current political issue, if a student cannot engage in critical listening, they may not be able to assess their classmate's argument accurately. Without critical listening skills, the student may make biased judgments, respond emotionally, and form opinions in isolation from the opinions of others. By investing in critical listening skills, the student is more likely to understand the issue from multiple perspectives, engage with the perspectives of their peers,

The 4 Pillars of Critical Thinking

and develop more in-depth insights into the issue. Ultimately, developing critical listening skills can lead to a more effective critical thinking process where multiple perspectives can be heard and understood.

Likewise, self-removal is also an effective way of promoting better critical thinking when engaging with others. When engaging in critical thinking, removing oneself from their perspective is important to avoid bias. Self-removal from one's perspective allows for consideration of alternative points of view and ensures that focusing on all the relevant facts is maintained. It helps to focus on pertinent details without having to be drawn in by personal feelings related to the topic. Plus, it encourages a balanced review of data and eliminates subjectivity.

For the most part, self-removal offers a more impartial outlook that is less clouded by personal feelings and prejudices. It encourages greater creativity and open-mindedness and reduces the risk of overlooking potential solutions. Removing oneself from one's perspective when engaging in critical thinking is crucial because it helps ensure that all viewpoints are considered and that decisions are based on facts rather than emotion. It can provide more balanced insight and evaluate a problem or situation more accurately and productively.

Lastly, learn to embrace conflict and have different viewpoints. Embracing conflict is a key factor in critical thinking and personal development. Conflict is a natural part of life, and you cannot avoid it completely. Learning to embrace conflict and not be afraid of it is important. By doing this, you can become a better problem solver and increase your understanding of interacting effectively with others.

Embracing conflict helps improve critical thinking skills by providing an opportunity for discussion and debate. Debate forces us to analyze and evaluate our ideas and those of others, which can be critical in forming an informed opinion on an issue. It helps us to gain a deeper understanding of how to see things from multiple perspectives and to reach a well-rounded and unbiased decision. Using our critical thinking skills and understanding of various perspectives, we can better identify the root causes of problems and come to practical solutions. Confronting a problem head-on also helps build confidence as we take ownership of the problem and create our solutions.

Chapter 12:
Critical Thinking Exercises

Few skills are as important in our modern world as the ability to think critically. From the boardroom to the classroom, thinking critically is essential in every facet of life. *But how exactly do we go about improving this skill?* We have already talked about what critical thinking is and its many nuances. However, more than just understanding what it is, we need to actively take the time to develop and sharpen this skill as we grow older. This chapter will explore tips and exercises designed to enhance your critical thinking abilities and make you a more successful problem solver. Together, let us unlock the power of critical thinking and its potential to make you a better thinker and doer.

Working on Puzzles

Puzzles allow engaging with complex problems and help develop critical thinking skills. They require a combination of problem-solving, inductive reasoning, creative thinking, and pattern recognition. These are skills that can be used in other areas of life.

Challenging puzzles can help improve the ability to think abstractly. By manipulating the puzzle pieces, problem solvers are forced to use deductive logic and think in a more abstract, non-linear way. Through understanding how pieces fit together, how patterns are created, and how tasks can be broken down into smaller pieces, critical thinking skills are developed.

Complex puzzles also require a great deal of focus. As people have to work hard to deduce the answer to a puzzle, their ability to concentrate on the task without getting distracted is improved. Working on puzzles can also help to improve problem-solving strategies. As different puzzles require different methods of solving, the skill of problem identification and applying the right strategy is developed. By repeatedly intensely focusing on puzzles, the ability to cultivate concentration skills is improved.

In addition, puzzles allow applying existing knowledge in a novel context. As the puzzle's complexity increases, the problem-solver has to draw upon past knowledge and combine it with analytical thinking skills to progress. Therefore, the perception of patterns and the ability to think logically are developed, increasing the level of critical thinking skills.

Numerical puzzles like Sudoku are perfect for sharpening mathematical ability. These puzzles involve recognizing patterns, combining logic and mathematical knowledge, and prioritizing certain numbers over others. Numerical puzzles also come with various difficulty levels to accommodate learners of any age and level of knowledge.

Another type of puzzle is a word puzzle. Word puzzles range from crossword puzzles and word searches to anagrams and scrambles. These puzzles are great for improving word recognition and expanding vocabulary, as they encourage the mind to think of creative solutions.

Puzzles come in various shapes and sizes, ranging from simple connect-the-dot exercises to complex, multidimensional challenges. The difficulty of puzzles can also be adjusted to the individual's skill level, allowing people to move from easier to more challenging puzzles at their own pace. This lets problem-solvers learn from their mistakes and increases their sense of self-efficacy, making them more confident in their problem-solving and critical-thinking abilities.

Reading Critically

Reading critically can improve one's critical thinking abilities by helping one to analyze, evaluate, and interpret the material in a more meaningful and deeper way. Reading critically involves finding gaps in content, inconsistencies, and other errors that the author or writer may have overlooked. When reading critically, a reader should ask questions such as *"what assumptions is the author making?" "what evidence is the author relying on?"* and *"are any of the conclusions unsupported?"*

For example, when reading an article on the impacts of global warming, a reader should look for evidence that supports the author's argument, such as peer-reviewed studies, data from reputable sources, or research conducted by experts in the field. A reader should also consider what evidence may have been overlooked or neglected in the author's argument. The reader should also be asking themselves if the conclusions drawn by the author are supported by the evidence provided or if any of the evidence is contradictory or unsubstantiated.

Staying current on the events and news in their field of interest provides a useful platform for critical thinking. That is why staying updated on news stories and developing rational opinions around them can go a long way in developing one's aptitude for logic and reasoning. But it is not enough to merely be reading these articles and journals. It is also important to use these sources to facilitate discussions with others. Keeping an eye out for new opinions, solutions, and methods can help offer new perspectives and aid in developing critical thinking skills. The act of actively engaging in conversation with peers about the events in their field can help a person become exposed to various opinions and insights, allowing for a better understanding of the situation and the potential solutions present.

Also, through a critical analysis of any text, a reader gains a deeper understanding of the material, allowing them to make more informed decisions in their everyday life. Reading critically encourages readers to think critically, which in turn helps them to evaluate and interpret any given material more effectively. It helps them to recognize patterns of evidence and any potential flaws in the argument, allowing them to draw more informed conclusions.

Reading comprehension and forming a reading habit both take effort and practice. One of the first steps is to read widely and deeply to enhance your reading comprehension. You can start by reading in areas of personal interest, including magazines, novels, or the local news. This will help expand your knowledge base and help hone your understanding of different writing styles. Additionally, engaging with the material by engaging in open-ended discussions and writing summaries of your reading is a great way to enhance your comprehension.

To form a reading habit, you must take the initiative to make time each day to set aside for reading. Ensure you are comfortable, free from distractions, and have a proper workspace. Over time, it will become easier to read and form a consistent reading routine. It might help to keep track of your reading progress and set rewards for yourself that you can enjoy upon reaching certain goals. Additionally, consider joining book clubs or discussion groups to help maintain your motivation and focus, which brings us to the following critical thinking exercise on this list.

Participating in Discussions or Debates

Participating in discussions and debates can help improve a person's critical thinking skills by forcing them to think creatively and critically while expanding their knowledge. When in a discussion or debate, an individual must take the time to analyze the information and evidence presented, evaluate arguments and positions, analyze one's beliefs, and recognize other people's positions and arguments. Additionally, discussing and debating with others allows people to look at a topic from multiple perspectives, uncover ideas that had not been explored, and deepen their understanding.

For example, say a person is discussing with someone else about the death penalty. The person's initial opinion may be that the death penalty is wrong. However, after debating the topic and hearing many arguments and evidence on both sides, they may learn more about the issue and arrive at a more complicated conclusion. They may understand why some people support the death penalty and the fallacies in the arguments against it. In the debate, they may find more evidence or points of view to challenge their views and drive further discussion. Ultimately, this thought process and exchange with the other person allows their critical thinking skills to expand and their understanding of the issue to deepen.

Due to the availability of technology and social media platforms, it is much easier for people to participate in civil discussions and debates than ever before. Technology has enabled instant access to vast amounts of information, allowing people to come to the discussion or debate much more informed and prepared to discuss their views intelligently. Furthermore, people can communicate and exchange ideas with people from around the world much more easily, allowing for a more diverse range of opinions and experiences to be heard in the conversation. With the help of technology and online platforms such as Reddit, Twitter, and message boards, people can engage in civil debates and discussions across the globe, making it much easier for them to enhance their critical thinking capabilities.

In addition, the rise of "fact-checking" websites has made it easier to ensure that statements made in debates or conversations are based on facts and that no false information is being passed as truth. This further promotes civil disputes by ensuring the discussion is based on facts instead of opinions or emotions.

For interactions to be productive and successful, people must be responsible and stay civil when engaging in discussions or debates with others, whether online or offline. By remaining courteous and respectful, individuals are more likely to remain open-minded and motivated to move towards potential solutions or compromise, even when disagreements occur. Individuals should approach conversations with an open mind and a goal of respectful dialogue. Avoiding personal attacks is key to keeping debates constructive. Even if an individual strongly disagrees with someone else's point of view, they should remain focused on ideas, issues, and facts.

It is also important to remain considerate of others' feelings during debates. Individuals should articulate their opinions in a way that is honest and direct while also being mindful of how they are framing their points of view. Refraining from sarcasm and offensive language is essential to demonstrate respect and a willingness to include other points of view.

Solving Practical Problems

Solving practical everyday problems can be a great way to enhance critical thinking skills, as it requires the problem-solver to think carefully about the problem and consider various solutions. Doing so requires the person to think through the problem from a logical perspective and multiple angles, understand the many factors that may have caused the problem, and evaluate the available data to come to a reasonable solution.

For example, if someone is having trouble starting their car, they must first analyze the situation. *What could be causing the vehicle not to start? Is it the battery, wiring, fuel system, or something else?* Once the possible causes have been identified, the person must evaluate the evidence further. *Have they had this problem before? Does the engine make any unusual sounds or smells? Does turning the key result in any noise?* Incorporating thought and observation into the problem-solving process can help to enhance critical thinking skills.

Another example is putting together an Ikea piece of furniture. Putting the time and thought into mastering the instructions can help to boost critical thinking skills. Simple tasks such as studying the diagram, picturing what each piece looks like and fits into, and understanding the language in the instructions can all give someone problem-solving practice. The more practice people have in solving problems, the more their critical thinking skills can be enhanced.

Everyday life has many opportunities to enhance one's critical thinking capabilities. Whether a person is at work, in school, or just participating in daily activities, there are always ways that one can improve their critical thinking skills. One of the most effective methods of enhancing these abilities is by actively questioning the information given and being willing to challenge the established thought process. Taking the time to ask "*why*" and "*how*" when presented with a situation allows a person to identify gaps in knowledge and think more critically about the information provided. Additionally, it is important to actively seek out new sources of information, using the internet and books to navigate complicated topics and develop new questions.

Pillar 4: Application

Application is the fourth pillar of critical thinking, and it involves using the knowledge and skills acquired from the first three pillars: foundation, process, and improvement. This pillar involves actively reaching a reasonable solution or a rational decision. One can identify and apply the most useful concepts and methods to a given situation through the application. Furthermore, the application also allows one to assess their understanding and performance, which is essential for growth and development.

Aside from that, the application involves identifying and interpreting patterns, trends, and relationships in a given situation. It also entails the capacity to develop and justify feasible solutions to problems or questions. Additionally, the application requires evaluating evidence and data, formulating a compelling argument or solution, and communicating conclusions or decisions clearly and concisely.

Moreover, the application is necessary for developing critical thinking skills. It enables one to apply the knowledge, understanding, and analysis gained through the first three pillars to real-world situations and problems. Through this process, one can develop the ability to think independently, develop creative solutions, and learn to work effectively with others. Similarly, it allows one to create the ability to use knowledge, comprehension, and analysis to solve problems and make informed decisions. Ultimately, it is a key component of the critical thinking process and is necessary to become more effective in daily life. Without application, knowledge resides in mind and is relegated to useless theory. As such, through the application, a theory can actively influence one's life and those of others.

Chapter 13:
Applying Critical Thinking in Daily Life

*D*o *you often struggle to make decisions? Are you constantly second-guessing yourself even when it seems like a no-brainer?* This lack of faith in your judgment may relate to your critical thinking skills. As such, this skill is involved in evaluating various options and can prove invaluable for complex decisions. Likewise, when it comes to finding success in life, one thing that helps give an edge is critical thinking. Once we learn how to apply it daily, making well-thought-out decisions becomes easier.

In Health and Wellness

Critical thinking skills are essential for achieving optimal health and wellness. It is important to think objectively and use analytical skills to make informed health decisions. We can apply critical thinking skills in health and wellness in various ways. One example is examining the evidence behind health claims. This requires us to research and digest the evidence to decide what is most beneficial for our health. It is important to remember to evaluate the source of any study or article, looking for contradictions and inconsistencies. Balancing these sources with an expert-backed opinion will provide a more balanced view of a recommendation.

Another example is developing a plan for our individual health needs. When it comes to health, every person's needs are different, and developing an individualized plan requires us to use critical thinking skills. It involves deeply analyzing our health needs and assessing our options. When creating a plan, it is essential to use logic and reasoning to ensure that it gives us a higher chance of success. Likewise, consider our circumstances and limitations, such as lifestyle, budget, and resource access.

At its core, critical thinking involves using evidence to draw conclusions or make decisions. When applied to health and wellness, this can help us make informed decisions tailored to our needs. It also helps us understand what our body is telling us and how to advocate for ourselves.

In the Workplace

Applying critical thinking in the workplace can help organizations make better decisions and achieve greater success. One way to apply critical thinking skills in the workplace is through problem-solving. Problem-solving requires individuals to analyze all the available information to develop the most effective solution to the problem. When attempting to solve a problem, it is important to consider various perspectives and weigh each potential solution's pros and cons before deciding. For example, if an organization needs to reduce costs, employees can use critical thinking skills to decide which areas to cut back on without adversely affecting the business.

Creativity is another way to apply critical thinking skills in the workplace. Thinking critically can help individuals develop innovative ideas that may not have previously been considered. When employing creative thinking, individuals should consider various possibilities and think outside the box. For example, if a company attempts to increase sales, it can use creative ideas to develop a unique marketing strategy to help it stand out from the competition.

In Education

Critical thinking is an invaluable skill in education and academics. The critical thinking process enables learners to make informed decisions and gain deeper knowledge. It also helps students solve problems and understand how to apply existing knowledge to new scenarios.

There are several ways to facilitate critical thinking in the classroom. Firstly, teachers should provide students with a wide range of resources and materials to access information and evidence. This could include textbooks, online educational tools, newspapers, and historical documents. This material gives students the necessary information to form conclusions and draw their own ideas about any subject matter.

Another way to apply critical thinking skills in an educational setting involves engaging in class discussions. When participating in class discussions, critical thinking skills are needed to take note of the different perspectives on a topic being discussed, reflect on those perspectives, and evaluate the implications of those perspectives on the topic. For example, suppose a class discusses decriminalizing certain drugs, such as marijuana. In that case, students need to be able to consider the different perspectives on the topic, such as the potential social and economic benefits of decriminalizing marijuana as well as the potential public health, legal, or safety implications of decriminalizing marijuana.

In addition to class discussion, critical thinking skills can be applied in other educational settings, such as essays and written assignments. When writing essays or other assignments, critical thinking skills are needed to engage in systematic thought processes, strategically organize the assignment, and construct logically reasoned arguments. For example, suppose an essay prompt asks the student to consider the implications of a certain policy. In that case, the student needs to engage in critical thinking skills to reflect on the various perspectives of the policy, as well as evidence and sources that further explain the various implications of the policy.

In Personal Finance

In personal finance, critical thinking skills can be applied to many decisions and activities. One way to apply critical thinking skills to personal finance is when making purchase decisions. Whether it is a need or a want, asking yourself questions such as *"why do I want this?" "what are the benefits of getting it?"* and *"how will this affect my finances in the long run?"* can help you to make a more informed, rational decision. Spending your money wisely and considering each purchase's pros and cons can help you avoid financial regrets and make more mindful decisions.

Another way to apply critical thinking to personal finance is when considering different types of investments. Critical thinking skills are useful here to evaluate the investment options, such as stocks, bonds, REITs, ETFs, and mutual funds, to determine the best one for your financial goals. Using data-driven approaches to weigh each option's cost, risk, and return. Aside from that, critical thinking skills can be applied to developing a financial plan. Likewise, critical thinking skills are essential here to set clear goals, consider your financial situation, and devise a plan to reach your goals based on sound evidence and research. This can involve learning how to budget, invest, and set milestones that are specific, measurable, achievable, relevant, and timely (SMART).

The 4 Pillars of Critical Thinking

In Personal Relationships

While it is easy to see critical thinking as a skill that only applies to leadership, business, or academic pursuits, that is not always the case. It is not just an academic exercise but a crucial skill in many aspects of our life, including personal relationships. Applying critical thinking skills in our interpersonal relationships allows us to assess the viability of arguments, consider alternative perspectives, and make better decisions that can make for more harmonious relationships and social environments.

For example, critical thinking skills can be invaluable when dealing with conflictual situations with a friend or family member. By engaging in critical thinking, we consider both sides of the argument and reflect on whether our point of view is sound given all the relevant factors. Additionally, we may be more willing to empathize with the other person's perspective and explore additional alternatives. With this knowledge, we can make more informed decisions as we can better weigh and consider each option's pros and cons.

On a larger scale, we can apply critical thinking to develop our thoughts about ourselves and our relationship with others. A critical thinker might, for example, think about how others perceive them and what kind of impression the individual may be giving off. In examining the constituent elements of a healthy relationship, the critical thinker can think through both persons' actions, responses, and attitudes to better assess the quality of the relationship and make positive changes as necessary.

It is essential to recognize that critical thinking is a skill that needs to be exercised and further developed over time. Regular practice, assessment, and improvement of one's critical thinking skills are key to making skillful and beneficial relationship decisions. Practicing critical thinking allows us to make better and wiser decisions, communicate our intentions more effectively, and establish healthier and more meaningful connections.

Conclusion

Thinking critically is vital for making the most effective decisions possible and can help lead one to a more successful and satisfying life. Developing the skills to question assumptions and challenge the status quo can help ensure we pursue truths instead of merely accepting them. Throughout this book, we have explored the benefits of being open to different ideas and perspectives and learning to look at the world with a critical eye. Armed with these skills and this greater understanding of how to think more critically, we can actively shape our future and create a world of limitless possibilities.

Breaking the art of critical thinking into four pillars made grasping such a complex and nuanced topic easy and digestible. Of course, not everyone will be able to achieve the same level of critical thinking. But everyone always has the potential to improve their ability to think reasonably and logically. Everyone has the potential to fight their own biases and prejudiced assumptions. Everyone has the capacity for improvement in the realms of self-awareness and reflection. We could all benefit from learning more about the foundations, processes, improvement techniques, and applications of critical thinking.

After learning about the four pillars of critical thinking, it is important to remember that applying those thoughts to your everyday life is essential for growth and success. Our foundation must be strong to move forward with process and improvement to bring our thought patterns to fruition. While not all paths of thought lead to success, the journey will undoubtedly provide you with personal growth and insight into yourself.

Aside from applying these thoughts and concepts to your life, it is also important to spread its message to those you care deeply about. When one person can think more critically for themselves, the entire world can also benefit from it. Do not be afraid to encourage your family, friends, peers, and loved ones to pursue this path of enlightened thinking. Critical thinking allows people to think more deeply and evaluate arguments and facts. This type of thinking helps them think more objectively and look at multiple perspectives to reach a more informed decision that can benefit everyone involved. This skill can help to resolve conflicts and lead to better decision-making and discussions around important social issues.

This book has offered valuable insight into critical thinking and how its practice can help you lead a more fulfilling life. By recognizing and understanding the four pillars of critical thinking, we are more aware of our approach to thought and how that affects our day-to-day actions. Most importantly, this book has offered an important takeaway that can benefit anyone's life: *You have the power to shape your thought processes and, ultimately, a better future. Any success you look to achieve in life can only come from empowering yourself to think independently and critically.*

Glossary

Analyze: To examine in detail to draw conclusions or gain understanding.

Assumption: An unstated belief or condition that affects the outcome of a situation.

Bias: A prejudice in favor of or against something.

Conclusion: Findings after considering all available evidence, analyzing the facts and data, exploring and evaluating the alternatives, and making an informed decision. The final step in the critical thinking process.

Corroborate: To confirm or support with evidence or testimony.

Creativity: Generating ideas or solutions to problems that are novel and useful.

Critical thinking: The ability to think clearly and effectively, analyze accurately, and reach sound decisions based on evidence.

Debate: A structured discussion on a topic with two or more sides.

Deductive reasoning: A logical process that begins with a general statement and is narrowed down to specific conclusions by applying facts and evidence.

Evidence: Facts and data which support a particular view.

Fact: A statement that is proven to be true.

Fallacy: An error in reasoning that hinders or undermines an argument's validity or soundness.

Hypothesize: To form an idea or explanation based on incomplete evidence.

Inductive reasoning: A type of reasoning that goes from specific facts or observations to general conclusions or theories.

Inference: A conclusion reached from evidence or premises.

Insight: The ability to see or understand the inner nature of a problem or situation.

Logic: The process of using rules of reasoning to draw conclusions and solve problems.

Objectivity: The ability to evaluate a situation or argument without influence from one's opinion or feelings.

Open-mindedness: The willingness to try out new ideas and approach problems from different points of view.

Perception: The process of interpreting sensory information to assign meaning to it.

Perspectives: Different points of view which take into account the interests and opinions of others.

Prejudice: A preconceived opinion or attitude not based on reason or experience, typically involving negative feelings.

Premise: A statement or idea which serves as the basis for a conclusion or argument.

The 4 Pillars of Critical Thinking

Principle: A fundamental truth or law which provides a basis for decision-making.

Reflection: Considering or reconsidering a topic or idea with a fresh perspective and openness.

Self-awareness: Having an awareness of one's own emotions and behavior and how it might affect others.

Subjective: An opinion or statement not based on facts or evidence.

Theory: An organizing principle that draws connections between different elements.

References

Baruch Fischhoff. (2013). *Judgment and decision making*. Routledge.

Bowell, T., Cowan, R., & Kemp, G. (2020). *Critical thinking: a concise guide*. London And New York Routledge.

Cherry, K. (2020). *How cognitive biases influence how you think and act*. Verywell Mind. https://www.verywellmind.com/what-is-a-cognitive-bias-2794963

Childs, D. (2019). *What makes valid research? How to verify if a source is credible on the internet*. Democracy and Me. https://www.democracyandme.org/what-makes-valid-research-how-to-verify-if-a-source-is-credible-on-the-internet/

Coyne, T. (2020). *Three techniques for weighing evidence: A short guide*. Www.linkedin.com. https://www.linkedin.com/pulse/three-techniques-weighing-evidence-short-guide-tom-coyne/?trk=read_related_article-card_title

Glaser, E. (1942). An Experiment in Development of Critical Thinking. *Teachers College Record: The Voice of Scholarship in Education*, *43*(5), 1–18. https://doi.org/10.1177/016146814204300507

Haddad, A. (2019). *Cultural bias - an overview*. Www.sciencedirect.com. https://www.sciencedirect.com/topics/medicine-and-dentistry/cultural-bias

Halpern, D. (2014). *Thought and knowledge: An introduction to critical thinking*. Psychology Press.

Iacurci, G. (2022). *Women are still paid 83 cents for every dollar men earn. Here's why*. CNBC. https://www.cnbc.com/2022/05/19/women-are-still-paid-83-cents-for-every-dollar-men-earn-heres-why.html

Indeed Team. (2023). *21 different types of evidence used in jury trials*. Indeed Career Guide. https://www.indeed.com/career-advice/career-development/different-types-of-evidence

James, M. (2019). *What is statistical significance?* Investopedia. https://www.investopedia.com/terms/s/statistical-significance.asp

Leary, J. D., & Robinson, R. (2018). *Post traumatic slave syndrome : America's legacy of enduring injury and healing*. Joy Degruy Publications Inc.

MacKnight, C. (2001). *Teaching critical thinking through online discussions*. https://er.educause.edu/-/media/files/article-downloads/eqm0048.pdf

Mandalios, J. (2013). RADAR: An approach for helping students evaluate internet sources. *Journal of Information Science, 39*(4), 470–478. https://doi.org/10.1177/0165551513478889

Marr, B. (2022). *13 easy steps to improve your critical thinking skills*. Forbes. https://www.forbes.com/sites/bernardmarr/2022/08/05/13-easy-steps-to-improve-your-critical-thinking-skills/

Mitchell, K. L. (2020). Taking steps to address racial disparities in sentencing. *Federal Sentencing Reporter, 33*(1-2), 22–26. https://doi.org/10.1525/fsr.2020.33.1-2.22

Performance Management Consultants. (n.d.). *What is critical thinking and why is it valuable in the workplace?* PMC Training. https://pmctraining.com/site/resources-2/what-is-critical-thinking-and-why-is-it-valuable-in-the-workplace/

Schmicking, D. (2014). *Handbook of phenomenology and cognitive science*. Springer.

Shatz, I. (n.d.). *Hanlon's razor: Why you shouldn't start by assuming the worst*. Effectiviology. https://effectiviology.com/hanlons-razor/

Stafford, T. (2022). *Developing an effective root cause analysis in healthcare*. Performance Health Partners. https://www.performancehealthus.com/blog/developing-an-effective-root-cause-analysis

Study.com. (2023). *Convergence of evidence: Meaning & importance*. Study.com. https://study.com/academy/lesson/convergence-of-evidence-meaning-importance.html#:~:text=The%20convergence%20of%20evidence%20refers

Tomaszewski, M. (2019). *Top 8 critical thinking skills and ways to improve them*. Zety. https://zety.com/blog/critical-thinking-skills#:~:text=Interpretation%3A%20concluding%20what%20the%20meaning

Tuts Master. (2021). *Characteristics of critical and uncritical thinkers.* TutsMaster; TutsMaster. https://tutsmaster.org/characteristics-of-critical-and-uncritical-thinkers/

Tversky, A., & Kahneman, D. (1973). Availability: A heuristic for judging frequency and probability. *Cognitive Psychology, 5*(2), 207–232.

Tversky, A., & Kahneman, D. (1974). Judgment under uncertainty: Heuristics and biases. *Science, 185*(4157), 1124–1131. https://doi.org/10.1126/science.185.4157.1124

University of Pittsburgh Communications Services Webteam. (2015). *Argument: Claims, reasons, evidence.* Pitt.edu; University of Pittsburgh. https://www.comm.pitt.edu/argument-claims-reasons-evidence

Wilson, P. F., Dell, L. D., & Anderson, G. F. (1993). *Root cause analysis.* Asq Press.

Made in the USA
Middletown, DE
23 October 2024